OPENING THE BIBLE WITH CHILDREN

Beginning Bible Skills

Opening the Bible With Children

Patricia Griggs

A Griggs Educational Resource

Abingdon Press / Nashville

To the students and staff of the
Lower School
at St. Catherine's School in Richmond, Virginia, in gratitude for the
opportunity to teach and grow with them.

OPENING THE BIBLE WITH CHILDREN
Copyright © 1986 by Abingdon Press

Second Printing 1987

This book is printed on acid-free paper.

Library of Congress Cataloging-in-Publication Data

GRIGGS, PATRICIA, 1935-
    Opening the Bible with children
    (A Griggs educational resource)
    Bibliography: p.
    1. Bible--Children's use. 2. Bible--Study. I. Title.
BS618.G75   1986   220'.07   85-30633

ISBN 0-687-29210-7   (pbk. : alk. paper)

Scripture text and illustration are from the *Good News Bible*, the Bible in Today's English Version. Copyright © American Bible Society 1966, 1971, 1976. Used by permission.

MANUFACTURED BY THE PARTHENON PRESS AT
NASHVILLE, TENNESSEE, UNITED STATES OF AMERICA

CONTENTS

_____

INTRODUCTION

Each time I teach church school (regardless of the age group), I am faced with several tasks:

First, *the task of using the curriculum in such a way that the students are able to reach as many of my objectives as possible for each session.*

Second, *the task of helping students gain access to the Bible by learning simple Bible skills.*

Third, *the task of creating in my classroom a community of faith that enables students to open up to one another, to me, to themselves, and to God.*

Fourth, *the task of communicating my faith to my students through my relationship with each of them.*

The task I have decided to focus on in this book is the task of opening the Bible with children through Bible skills. This task has been chosen because there are few resources which supply the teacher of children with activities and guidelines to do this job. While some curriculum resources spend several weeks in the fall dealing with basic Bible skills, little is written with a conscious effort to incorporate the teaching and the use of Bible skills throughout the year. The teacher may approach teaching Bible skills several ways—by putting the curriculum aside, teaching Bible skills for several weeks, then going back to the curriculum; by assuming that the students in the class already know basic Bible skills, thus not taking a significant amount of time teaching them; or by making a conscious effort to find resources that will help in the teaching of Bible skills and trying to incorporate those skills into the curriculum that is being used.

I have found that spending a few weeks in September on Bible skills is not enough and is not always effective for several reasons:

—There are always children who are not present every Sunday and need to catch up when they return.

—The skills need to be used over and over if they are to be learned.

—Sometimes the children I am teaching are not ready for such a unit of study in the fall, but are more ready for it later in the year. This means rearranging the order of the lessons.

I have become an advocate for integrating the teaching of Bible skills with the regular curriculum so that students are involved in using these skills all year long. While it may seem easier to spend several weeks teaching Bible skills, then continuing with the regular curriculum, this may not be the most educationally sound approach. The best way to learn Bible skills is to use them over and over again in a purposeful way. This approach to teaching means that the teacher must make some adjustments in using the curriculum. It means being continually alert to opportunities for the students to use and to practice particular skills, and being able to create activities which involve the students in using the skill(s). While this may be more work for the teacher, it is much more advantageous to the learner.

For the last several years, I have kept the resources developed during my teaching so that I could share them with you through this book. In addition to sharing these resources with you, I will attempt to share my ideas and experiences in the hope that they will help you as you do your planning.

Teachers of children who read will find this book more helpful than teachers of non-readers. While teachers of non-readers are addressed, the activities in later chapters require that children be able to read.

I have had two experiences in recent years that have been significant in providing the opportunity to create many of the resources you will find on the following pages.

One experience I had was teaching a class of second and third-graders at the Second Presbyterian Church in Richmond, Virginia. My students were the proud recipients of the gift of Bibles from the church. I asked for this class because I knew they would receive Bibles that year, and I wanted to see what challenges this event presented to the teacher. Our Director of Christian Education, Martha Osborne, was interested in my quest for this experience and encouraged me to experiment and to be as creative as I could in my teaching. Out of that year came many of the examples and stories I will be sharing with you. I had the opportunity to explore the meaning of the event for the children, and I was challenged to channel their enthusiasm so that the receiving of a Bible would nurture their love for the Bible and would help them grow in their faith.

The second significant experience was the teaching of Bible and religion at St. Catherine's School in Richmond, Virginia. I had the joy of teaching grades one through five (two classes at each grade level, each week). Each child came to my class once a week. Classes were from 35 to 50 minutes long, depending on the grade level. There were from 19 to 23 students per class.

The big difference between teaching in church and in school was that the children were more regular in attendance at school; they were responsible for homework, and I was responsible for measuring their progress and giving them grades. The advantage for me was that I was teaching in the midst of the students' academic program. I could easily see what was being taught in other subjects at each grade level. I was also seeing several grade levels of children each day and all levels each week, which enabled me to compare the abilities of the children in both the conceptual and the skill areas.

I did a lot of experimenting to test out the theories I had read about to see if my own ideas about what children can and cannot do were valid. The results of this experimentation are reflected in the recommendations and ideas that appear in the following chapters.

Another concern which I wish to address is the practice of giving Bibles to children in a particular grade each year. This is a good tradition that might be made more meaningful and memorable if those responsible were to take a fresh look at what they are doing and why. The giving of Bibles can be, and should be, a significant part of the educational program of the church, and a significant and meaningful time for the recipients. I would like to give some suggestions that will help persons evaluate what they are doing so they can take that fresh look. Related to this concern is the question of Bible selection. We are constantly asked questions such as: *"Which translation is the best one to use in church school?" "I want to give a Bible to my child. Which one should I give?" "Is there a good children's Bible that is written for beginning readers?"* To respond to these questions, I have included a short section on Bible translations that I hope will be helpful to those who are confused when they walk into a book store and see all the translations that are available.

The most advantageous way to use this book is to read it through once so that you become familiar with what is here and with the approach I am taking to teaching Bible skills. Then, go back to those sections of the book that will help you most in your particular situation. I caution you to resist going straight to the activities section. Although that section may be helpful as you do your lesson planning, the guidance you need in order to choose appropriate activities appears in the earlier chapters.

OPENING THE BIBLE WITH CHILDREN

OPEN—

having no enclosing or confining barrier . . .
not shut or locked . . .
completely free from concealment . . .
exposed to general view or knowledge . . .
exposed or vulnerable to attack or question . . .
not covered . . .
not restricted to a particular group or category of participants . . .
spread out—unfolded . . .
willing to hear and consider or to accept and deal with . . .
to make available for entry or passage by . . . removing (as a cover), or
clearing away (as an obstruction) . . .

—Webster's Ninth New Collegiate Dictionary

When we talk about opening the Bible with children, we are referring to the revealing of the scriptures by removing barriers to understanding and exposing what is there so that children can enter the scriptures and explore what they find. We are also talking about a teacher who is "open." An open teacher is one who questions, who accepts the doubts of children, who is willing to struggle with the students as values are formed and foundations of faith established, and who is willing to allow children to have beliefs that can change with time. When we open the Bible with children, we are opening up the opportunity to discover and explore our relationship with God. We are making it possible for students to make decisions that will form the foundations of their lives as Christians in today's world.

Adults are often anxious to share the Bible with children and to teach them all about God, Jesus, and important people in the Old and New Testaments. We often forget that the Bible is a book written about, by, and for adults. We want it to be for children, too, so we begin introducing them to the Bible from the time they are infants. What I hope to do in this book is to help teachers and parents think about what is appropriate for children as we consider their various abilities and needs at different developmental stages. It is hoped that we will see there is no harm in slowing down our pace of introducing the Bible and working for quality in what we are doing rather than the quantity of what we can do in a year's time.

Many children have an awareness of God before they know what a Bible is. When I think back on my childhood, I can remember wondering about God before I was aware of the Bible and of Bible stories. When I was six, one of my aunts gave me a Bible story book (which I still have). This was my first exposure to the Bible. These short stories, verses, and brightly colored pictures made a lasting impression on me.

9

For many children, encounters with the Bible begin at an early age, before they are able to read or fully comprehend what the Bible is. If a child grows up in a Christian family, it is possible that he or she will see the Bible at home and hear mother or father read from it. The child will realize from the attitude of the parent that this is a special book. The child may come to associate this book with the word *God*.

In pre-school classes the teacher may hold an open Bible on the lap while telling a story. The words *God, Jesus, love,* and *care* may begin to be associated with this book. During these early years, a sense of mystery and awe may be developed in the child.

As children grow older, the teacher may tell them that "this story is from the Bible." The teacher may begin to use the words *New Testament* and *Old Testament*. While they do not fully understand what these words mean, the children become aware that there are two parts to the Bible. As they hear stories about God and Jesus, the children may begin to make some connections between the stories and the way they live.

Children's Bible storybooks may be introduced between the ages of four and six, not so that children can read them, but so that they can look at the large, colorful pictures while the teacher or parent reads or tells the stories. The pictures will influence the child's concepts of God and Jesus and will have much to do with what the child remembers about the story. For these reasons, choosing such books should be done with great care.

Even though children are beginning to read in the second grade (some very well), we must remember that being able to read a word and being able to understand that same word are two different things. We must not be fooled into thinking that because a child can read a story from the Bible that child also comprehends the story. Work still needs to be done on defining words and concepts and carefully choosing short verses to be read.

Beginning readers are excited about reading and want to see the words the teacher reads. They often want to do the reading themselves. It is good to allow children to read aloud, but it is important that it be done after the teacher has presented the story, and after difficult words are defined and pronunciation has been worked on. When we allow a beginning reader to introduce a story to the class, the children who are listening may become impatient with the reader. Poor reading can make a story dull and cause students to lose interest. The reader can also become discouraged if the words are too difficult and can become embarrassed if the reading cannot be done well.

Third-graders are capable of reading and understanding many of the stories in the Bible. These children are enthusiastic about using the Bible themselves. They don't want the teacher to be the only one holding the Bible and reading from it. They want to follow along as it is read, and to do some of the reading for themselves. Third-graders are ready to begin developing simple, basic Bible skills.

Fourth, fifth, and sixth-graders are able and ready to learn about the formation of the Bible, develop more complicated Bible skills, begin using Bible resources, and use their newfound ability to think abstractly. These children are ready for Bible study and ready to apply what they read to their own lives.

I purposely titled this chapter "Opening the Bible *with* Children." The word *with* is important because it indicates that both the student and the teacher are involved in discovering more about God, our faith, and all that scripture holds for us. The journey of faith is not something we do alone, but a journey we experience in community. Although it is true that the teacher does generally know more about the Bible than does the student, it is also true that the teacher does not know everything and is a learner along with the students. When we do something *for* someone else, the other person does not necessarily have to become involved. All that is required of the person is to receive what we offer—and the person has a choice of whether to accept what we offer or not to accept it. When we do something *with* someone, both of us are involved together. It is through involvement and interaction that students learn.

CHURCHES GIVE BIBLES TO CHILDREN

A couple of months ago, I attended a very special service at church. I knew it was going to be special when I walked into the church and saw several stacks of new Bibles on the communion table. During the service the pastor, the fourth-grade teachers, and the elder related to the children's department came forward. The children in the fourth-grade class were called forward. Their excitement was electric. They stood around the table—eyes glued on the Bibles. The pastor spoke to them about the time when he, like them, stood in the front of the church to receive his Bible. He told them what that Bible has meant to him, what he expected them to do with their new Bibles, and that he hoped the Bible would have a significant influence on their lives.

After several minutes of well chosen words from the pastor, the elder and the teachers joined the pastor in presenting a new Bible to each child. I noticed that every one of them opened the new Bible immediately after returning to the group. All were looking at the inscription that had been written especially for them on the inside cover. As the prayer was being offered after the Bibles had been passed out, most of the children stood with their arms crossed, hugging the Bibles to their chests.

When the children returned to their seats, the first thing they did was to show the Bible to the person sitting next to them. I observed that most of the children got a hug and a big smile from someone sitting by them.

When it was time for the scripture reading, the pastor took the time to call attention to the scripture reference and encouraged people to find the reference using the Bibles in the pews—and the children to use the Bibles they had just received. He was careful this day to read from the same translation of the Bible that had been given to the children.

This service was special not only for the children who received their Bibles, but also for the whole congregation. Many people were reminded of the day they stood, like these children, at the front of the church to receive their first Bibles. Some people felt good that the church gave this significant gift to the children. Others were reminded of the value of the Bible and were glad that the book would find its way into the homes of these children, perhaps influencing more people in the family. Children are generally very excited about receiving the Bible. The first thing they want to do is read it. Often they want to start at Genesis 1:1 and read straight through. This can pose some problems. Children often get discouraged and stop reading because the language is difficult and because many of the words are unfamiliar. Some are surprised, fascinated, and disturbed by the stories in the beginning of Genesis.

Several years ago, I heard of one parent who called the church a few weeks after her third-grade son had received his Bible. Apparently the boy had been faithful in his reading and had made his way through a good part of the beginning of Genesis. The trouble was that he was now having nightmares because the stories he had read portrayed a vengeful God and wicked people. He became frightened. The parent was faced with a very difficult situation because neither her son nor she had received any direction for selecting stories to read.

CHURCHES GIVE BIBLES TO CHILDREN

There are several factors that influence children to start reading at Genesis 1 with the idea that they will read straight through the Bible.

1. **This is the way they have been taught to read other books—from page one to the end.**

2. **They may not know that the Bible is a collection of many books and that these books are not all in chronological order.**

3. **They may not have the skills required to look up and find particular stories that they remember and want to read.**

4. **They may not have learned how the Bible is structured. Types of literature and the way the books are grouped into sections will be taught when the children are older.**

5. **No suggestions have been made to the child about what should be read immediately after receiving the Bible.**

Teachers and parents who are alert to the implications of giving children Bibles without giving directions for reading will be careful to see that each child is given carefully selected passages to read for several weeks or even months after the class receives Bibles.

Teachers should be sure that some work has been done to prepare the children to receive their Bibles, and to follow up after the Bibles are presented. The class might be led to understand that the Bible is a collection of books, like a library, and it is not necessary to read the Bible from the beginning to the end like other books. There will be included in the curriculum some study of the formation of the Bible and its structure. Plans will be made for ways to make this gift from the church special and meaningful for the child so that an appreciation for the Bible is nurtured.

In preparation for giving Bibles, the church needs to ask:

1. **Why are we giving Bibles to the children?**
2. **What translation is best for these children?**
3. **When, during the year, should we present the Bibles?**
4. **How will we help teachers and parents prepare for this event and follow up afterward?**

Let us consider each of these questions in more depth.

WHY ARE WE GIVING BIBLES TO THE CHILDREN?

There are a number of reasons why a church might include this custom in its yearly schedule of events.

—*We have always done it—it is a tradition.*

—*We think it is a good way for the church to show the children that we think they are special and we care about them.*

—*Parents expect us to give the Bibles each year and would be upset if we did not do it this year.*

—*The children have older brothers or sisters who have received Bibles in past years and would be hurt and think it unfair if we stopped giving Bibles and they did not receive one.*

—*Children like to bring their own Bibles to church.*

—*Our teaching is more meaningful when the children are using their own Bibles.*

—*We can ask children to read a story, or have devotions, or prepare ahead of time at home if we know they have their own Bibles with which to work.*

Add your own reasons . . .

When we know why we are giving the Bibles to children, we can then consider whether our reasons, and the ages of the children to whom we are giving the Bibles, are consistent. If we are giving the Bible simply because to do so is a tradition and we think it is a good tradition, that is fine. These reasons make it appropriate to give them at any age. If, however, we are expecting the children to use the Bibles in a variety of ways, we should be sure we are giving Bibles which enable the children to accomplish what we have planned for them, and that guidance is given to help them to work on our objectives.

It is possible that we should consider giving our children Bibles a couple of times in their lives for different reasons. A list of appropriate times to give Bibles follows. Look at the list. Do you see some new ideas here worth considering for your church? Does looking at this list help you to form ideas to add to this list?

First or second grade. We might consider giving an illustrated Bible storybook to these children because we want them to have a gift from the church that communicates to them that the church cares about them. The Bible storybook is chosen because it contains stories that are appropriate for this age group, it has illustrations that are attractive, it portrays the stories in a way that is consistent with the church's educational stance, it has a text that is bbsed on a translation of the Bible approved by the church, and it is written with a vocabulary that the child can understand.

Third or fourth grade. We may decide to give the *International Children's Version (New Testament)* to these children because we want them to have a New Testament that they can read on their own. This version is written with a third-grade vocabulary and is laid out in such a way that it is easy to read and use. One helpful feature is the highlighting of difficult words with definitions of these words at the bottom of the page. We would give this portion of the Bible to children because we want them to have one they can easily read.

Fourth or fifth grade. We may want to give these children a *Good News Bible* because they are ready to do some serious Bible study and are learning Bible skills that enable them to use the study helps in the Bible. They still need a Bible that uses a simpler vocabulary such as this version has. This Bible not only has an appropriate vocabulary for this age group, but it also has word lists, cross-references, short introductory articles at the beginning of each book, an outline of each book, footnotes, maps, and good illustrations. If we give this Bible, we expect the children to read and use it. Teachers can then work at helping students master basic Bibles skills.

Youth. Youth need a Bible that has footnotes, cross-reference notes, maps, a concordance, and other helps as well as a more advanced vocabulary. We might give such a Bible to our young people at the time of their confirmation. It would be a meaningful gift which recognizes the needs of youth and an important event in the lives of our young people. We should choose a Bible that is commonly used in our church for worship and study.

When we consider why we are giving the Bibles, and the age of students receiving the Bibles, another question arises.

WHAT TRANSLATION IS THE BEST ONE FOR THESE PARTICULAR CHILDREN?

The translation we choose is related to several factors:

—*The reading level of the students.*
—*The translation used most frequently in the church.*
—*The way we expect the students to use the Bible.*

Choosing a translation that is appropriate is not an easy task. In fact, pastors and educators are often asked by parents, grandparents, and friends of children to recommend a good translation of the Bible for them to give to a child. When we enter a bookstore, the shelves are filled with a variety of translations and paraphrases of the Bible. It seems as if every time we turn around there is another choice being presented to us. The question of choosing a translation is important enough to spend some time here exploring the subject of biblical translations.

Why are there so many different translations?
The first reason is obvious. The Old Testament was originally written in Hebrew and the New Testament was originally written in Greek. To communicate the content of the Bible to anyone who does not speak or read Hebrew or Greek, we must translate.

A second reason is that the Protestant Reformation encouraged the idea that ordinary people as well as scholars and church members should be able to read the Bible. Consequently, there has been a continual effort to translate the original Hebrew and Greek into the current languages of the people. Because the English language continues to change, and because scholars are understanding more as they continue to study the scriptures in Hebrew and in Greek, it is necessary to continue to produce new translations.

Another reason for more translations and paraphrases is that there are some who wish to have a Bible that supports a particular doctrinal or theological point of view.

When we look at these reasons for various translations and versions of the Bible, we can see why so many have developed over the years, and why there are so many differences among them. It is important to read the introduction to the Bible that you select in order to discern what the translators were trying to accomplish with their translation.

Some translators are committed to developing a Bible that renders as correctly as possible a word-for-word translation from the Hebrew and the Greek into English. They are less concerned with rendering concepts into a contemporary idiom. Ordinarily these translations, which are more literal, are also more difficult for young readers to read and understand. *The American Standard Version* of the Bible is a good example of this type of translation.

Other translators are more concerned with presenting, as accurately as possible, the appropriate English words for the original Hebrew and Greek, while at the same time seeking to communicate in a style and language that can be readily understood by today's readers. A good representation of this type of translation is the *Good News Bible*.

There are still other scholars who seek to develop a Bible that presents their interpretation of scripture as well as what they believe to be a faithful translation. They add words and concepts that are not in the original Hebrew and Greek. For these persons, it is more important to provide a contemporary, readable rendition of the Bible than an accurate translation. In a technical sense these are not translations, but rather are paraphrases of the Bible. A paraphrase may make interesting reading, but it can never be depended upon to present a reliable translation. The most familiar example of this type is *The Living Bible*.

When we read the introduction to a Bible, we are able to find out if it is a translation from the latest Hebrew and Greek manuscripts, if it is a revision of another translation, or if it is a paraphrase. We can determine the purpose of the translation and the credentials of the translators. This information will help us to decide whether or not a particular translation will meet our needs or the needs of the children for whom we are selecting the Bible.

How do you compare Bibles?

Making a good choice of a Bible (or Bibles) requires time and effort. As you look at a variety of Bibles, keep the following questions in mind:

1. *Was the translation done by an individual or a committee?* A committee translation usually shows less theological bias if it crosses denominational lines.

2. *Is the translation an authorized one or not?* Some translations have been given the official support of various denominational or ecumenical bodies.

3. *What is the purpose of the translation?* You will usually find this information in the introduction, or preface, of the Bible.

4. *Is the translation printed in different formats with different bindings?* If the book is to be used in a classroom, you may want a different format and binding than if it is to be used primarily for devotional reading.

5. *Is the translation printed in one column per page or two columns?* Which is easier for the children to read?

6. *What size is the type? How heavy is the paper?* It is easier for children to read larger type and to handle heavier paper. Students who are going to use the Bible for study will want to write in the margins. This is easier if the paper is not tissue-thin.

7. *Is the translation printed verse by verse, or are verses grouped into paragraphs?*

8. *How are chapter and verse numbers printed?* Some are found in the margins and some within the text. Some use very small numbers that are hard to find and read.

9. *What order is followed in printing the books of the Bible? Does the Bible contain the Apocrypha?*

10. *How are Old Testament quotations in the New Testament indicated?* Some translations use italics, some use quotation marks.

11. *Does the version print Jesus' words in red?* This may be helpful, but it does impose a printer's or scholar's interpretation on the reader.

12. *How are italics used?* Sometimes italics are used to indicate that these English words have no actual equivalent in the Hebrew or Greek but are necessary for good English. Other translations use italics to show where Greek includes emphasis. The introduction to the Bible should tell you what the italics mean.

13. *Does poetry appear as poetry, and prose as prose?* Some publications ignore the distinction, but the Scriptures include both poetry and prose.

14. *What kinds of study helps are included?*
    —Footnotes? —Dictionary?
    —Cross-reference notes? —Maps?
    —Concordance? —Articles before, after,
    —Word list? or within the text?
    —Art work?

15. *Does the English style reflect the King James Version, or is it contemporary English?*

16. *Is the translation a revision of an older one, or is it a completely new translation based on the original Greek and Hebrew?*

CHURCHES GIVE BIBLES TO CHILDREN

When the church is ready to choose a translation of the Bible to give to children as a gift, someone has to take the responsibility to make an informed choice. This person will want to go to a religious book store which has a wide variety of Bibles and look at them, keeping the above questions in mind. This person may want to make several copies of the following check list to use as different Bibles are evaluated. The check lists and other notes that have been made will be helpful references after returning home. Also be aware that many religious book stores have a chart which lists a variety of translations and graphically compares them. Looking at that chart can be helpful. Talking to the pastor of the church and sharing what has been found and discussing questions that have been raised because of the search can be helpful. Basic to the selection is knowing why the Bible is being given, how the Bible will be used, and to whom it will be given.

Check List

Name of Bible _____

1. Who did this translation? _____

2. Is the translation an authorized one? _____

3. What is the purpose of this translation? _____
_____

4. This Bible appears in a format and binding appropriate ____ not appropriate _____ for us.

5. The translation is printed in one column per page ____ two columns per page _____.

6. The size of the type is _____ is not _____ appropriate.

7. The paper is heavy _____ light _____ tissue _____ etc. _____.

8. Chapter and verse numbers are within the text _____ in the margins _____ easy to read _____ hard to read _____.

9. The Apocrypha is _____ is not _____ included.

10. The Old Testament quotations in the New Testament are indicated by italics _____ quotation marks _____.

11. Jesus' words are _____ are not _____ printed in red.

12. This translation uses italics to indicate _____
_____

13. Poetry and prose do _____ do not _____ appear as poetry and prose.

14. The following study helps are included:

_____ footnotes   _____ cross reference notes   _____ concordance
_____ word list   _____ art work   _____ dictionary
_____ maps   _____ articles

15. The style reflects the King James Version _____

    Contemporary English _____

16. This translation is a revision of an older translation _____. This is a completely new translation based on the original Greek and Hebrew _____.

17. The vocabulary used in this translation indicates a reading level of _____.

WHEN, DURING THE YEAR, SHOULD WE PRESENT THE BIBLES?

We want the presentation of the Bibles to be a special experience for the children. The way the Bibles are given out in church, the preparation the teacher does with the children before and after the service, and the parents' involvement will all contribute to the specialness of the event. Choosing the date for giving the Bibles is also a contributing factor. Here are some things to think about as you consider an appropriate time of the year to give the Bibles:

What about fall? Enthusiasm is high for church school. If Bibles are given in the fall, the students can use them all year. Both are good reasons for choosing fall. However, before deciding on fall, we need to think about what we intend to do with the Bibles after they are given. Are we expecting the children to be able to read them and to comprehend what is read? Are we expecting them to use some Bible skills? Which ones? Have they learned the necessary skills in school to be able to use the Bible skills we will be teaching? Do we know the students well enough in the fall to know what their skill levels are?

What about a special season of the church year? Sometimes churches like to present the Bibles at the beginning of Lent so that children can be encouraged to read, to think, and to pray during the Lenten season. Some give the Bibles on Palm Sunday, others at Pentecost. If we choose a special service dedicated to celebrating an event in the church year, the children will associate receiving the Bible with that celebration. Each time that church year celebration comes around (First Sunday in Lent, Palm Sunday, Pentecost, and so on), the children will remember, "This is when we received our Bibles."

What about the end of the year? A second or third-grader will have more ability by the end of the year and will be able to be more successful with reading. A question to consider if we choose this time of year is: "How much time do we have left in church school before summer break to work with the children and their new Bibles?" It may be a good idea to plan to have several weeks of church school left before summer break so that there is some time to deal with the initial enthusiasm the children have when they receive their Bibles. The receiving of a Bible is often a good excuse for the teacher to introduce some new Bible skills, to answer questions not dealt with before about the Bible, and to guide the students' reading in a more purposeful way. On the other hand, if we are giving illustrated Bible storybooks to young children to let them know the church cares about them, the children do not need a lot of time with church school in order to respond to the gift. By the same token, older children (youth) may view the receiving of Bibles as a climax to the year and may not need the extensive follow-up that younger students do.

The fact is that we will be using Bibles in our teaching regardless of whether they are the property of the church or of the students. The teacher will introduce appropriate skills throughout the year regardless of when the Bibles are received in a special church service. The time of the year when the Bible is received is important as it relates to the total experience the children are having in church and church school, and especially to the follow-up that parents and teachers do in order to channel and guide the enthusiasm that is generated when the gift is received.

HOW DO TEACHERS AND PARENTS RESPOND?

There are too many times when teachers and parents regard the giving of Bibles as something the church does separate from what happens in church school or at home. Many parents and teachers would like to become involved with the children and their new Bibles but do not know how. Teachers often feel they have a curriculum to teach and do not see how to plan time to deal with the new Bibles—especially for more than one Sunday. Parents sometimes feel inadequate to guide their children's reading of the Bible and assume that since the children are going to church

18

school, they are learning about the Bible and are receiving guidance with their reading. There are many ways that teachers and parents can be helped to support and nurture children during this important time.

1. Parent meetings

Before the children are given their Bibles, the director of Christian education (or the pastor if there is no DCE) may call a meeting of the parents and teachers of the children receiving Bibles. At this meeting, there is an explanation of why the Bibles are being given to this particular group. The Bible that has been chosen is shared along with the reasons for choosing this particular version. Information about the developmental stages can be shared so that parents and teachers are made aware of realistic expectations for these children. The teacher(s) may have met ahead of time to plan for activities that they will do with the students the first few weeks, along with the regular curriculum, to help them become acquainted with their new Bibles. These activities and plans are shared with the parents. A listing of scripture readings appropriate for this age group may be hanged out to the parents so that they might have something concrete to refer to as they read with their children each night or as the children ask the parents for suggestions of what to read in the Bible. A listing of scripture passages on which future lessons are based could be given to parents so that the stories could be read at home before the children encounter them in church school. Parents could be given suggestions of ways to encourage the use of the Bible at home. Some expamples are:

—*Read a passage along with the table grace each evening.*

—*Read with the child at bedtime.*

—*Follow up at home with activity sheets that the teacher may send home. (These could be crossword puzzles, word searches, vocabulary lists, and any number of activities that require the child to use the Bible. A variety of activities will be found in the next section of this book, some of which will be appropriate to use as take-home activities.)*

—*Give the child a list of appropriate stories for reading. The list should have the title of the story, the Bible reference, and a short statement that tells the child what the story is about.*

Some time could be spent during the parents' meeting to use the *brainstorming* technique to create a list of other activities that can be done at home to respond to and to encourage their children's exploration of the Bible.

Time should be allowed for parents to ask questions during the meeting. It is important for parents to feel that they are a part of the teaching team and to know that they have some responsibility to respond to the child's gift of a Bible. It is a fact that the parents' use of the Bible at home and their attitudes toward the Bible may have more to do with the child's response to it than anything we can do at church. If parents do not regard the Bible as being important to their lives and ministry, then their children are not likely to think it is all that important either. The more we can do to nurture, educate, and encourage parents, the more we will be helping the children.

2. Bible day at church

On Bible day, church members are encouraged to bring to church Bibles that are special to them. These Bibles can be placed on tables in the narthex so that persons can look at them as they arrive or leave the church. They might be labeled and placed on tables in the fellowship hall for persons to look at during the fellowship hour. I heard of one church that found Bible day to be so exciting that it has developed the day to include a church service which focuses on some aspect of the formation of the Bible or on the sharing of the Bible through missions. One year they used resources from the American Bible Society to explore how the Bible is being shared throughout the world.

3. A special time with the pastor

The pastor of the church is often looked up to with awe by the children. To some, he or she is a mystery—someone set apart, someone different. As the wife of a pastor who loves children and works hard at getting close to the children in the church, I think most pastors would welcome the opportunity to meet with a class outside the sanctuary to interact on the children's familiar turf. If church school meets at the same time as worship and you have only one pastor, it may take some creative thinking to figure out how your pastor can meet with your children. But if there are several pastors, or if worship and church school meet at different hours, it is possible to invite the pastor to your classroom.

There are several times when such a visit by the pastor would be appropriate. One time would be the Sunday before the children receive their Bibles. The pastor could come to share with the children what will happen in the church service, where they will stand, what will be said and done, and what will be expected of them. The children will become more relaxed about the service if they know what to expect and if they have had a relaxed and fun encounter with the pastor. The pastor might at this time also share some experiences with the Bible remembered from childhood or some recent experiences.

Another time to have a visit would be after the Bibles are received. The pastor might bring a variety of Bibles to class and let the children explore them to see how they are alike and how they are different. Maybe a Greek or Hebrew edition could be among the collection. Seeing these Bibles and hearing the pastor talk about them and maybe even reading something in Hebrew or Greek would make the Bible very special. It would be fun to teach the children to print and to say several words in Hebrew or Greek and to find these words in the Bible.

4. Children participating in worship

Whether your church has children attending for a part of the worship service or all of it will determine whether you can do any of the following. It is hoped that there will be opportunities for the children to participate regularly in your worship services.

—When scripture is being read during the service, take time to tell the congregation (even though it is listed in the bulletin) what the scripture passage will be and then allow time for persons to find it before the pastor begins to read. This will encourage the children to use their Bibles during worship and will help them to remember and to understand the scripture passage because they can see as well as hear the words.

—Consider occasionally letting a child read one of the scripture passages during the service. If the passage is given to the child ahead of time, and time is spent with the child practicing the reading at home and in the sanctuary (with the microphone if one is used), a child can do a very good job of reading the scripture.

—In many churches, Advent or Lenten candles are lit during these seasons. Often when the candles are lit, a scripture passage is read. A child could light the candle(s) and read the scripture passage.

—Special activity sheets related to the worship service can be prepared for children to use during the service. They can be picked up or given out as the children enter the sanctuary. I visited a church recently where a box of medium-sized manila envelopes had been prepared and placed in the narthex. Each Sunday as the children came to church, they would take an envelope from this box. In it they found a number of items appropriate for that particular service. On the Sunday I attended this church, the envelope contained an activity sheet, a pencil, a small note pad, a couple of crayons, a bulletin (which had been especially marked for the participation of the children for this Sunday), and several bookmarks to be used to mark the hymns to be sung this Sunday. The bookmarks were all different colors, and each had a number (1,2,3, or 4) on it (the corresponding numbers had been printed by hand on the child's copy of the bulletin). On the outside of the envelope was a greeting and instructions which helped the child use what was in the envelope. The final instruction was for the envelope to be placed in the box after church so it could be prepared for the next Sunday.

The worship activity sheet may contain any number of activities:

1. A scripture passage upon which the sermon is based, along with several questions to be answered as the child listens to the sermon.

2. A crossword puzzle or word game using key words related to the theme of the service.

3. Instructions to compare a hymn with a passage of scripture. The child may do an activity to complete this comparison or may illustrate the message that is discovered while looking at the scripture and the hymn.

4. Instructions for searching through the bulletin to find all the places in the service where scripture is used and for identifying the form in which we encounter the scripture: Bible reading, hymn, anthem, congregational responses, prayers, and so on.

—Sunday school classes can prepare banners based on scripture passages that will be used in worship. The banners can be shared in worship in a variety of ways. During the opening hymn, several children can process with the banners and place them in stands along the walls of the church, or the banners can simply be hung and have attention called to them and the class that made them.

—When the scripture for the service is known several weeks ahead of time, children can create an illustration for the cover of the bulletin or several drawings can be shared as inserts in the bulletin.

We could go on and on finding ways children can be included in worship. This is not the subject of this book. But I hope the suggestions I have made will help you think about specific ways that we can connect the receiving of the Bible, the study of scriptures, and the experience of worship for children.

5. Special activities in the classroom

The previous examples all suggest that the teacher has become involved with the parents and the DCE or the pastor in planning for ways to make the giving and receiving of Bibles meaningful for the children. In addition to this planning, the teacher will want to plan activities in the classroom that will open the Bible with children and will encourage the learning of Bible skills. The next chapter focuses directly on this concern.

This is a good time to check on the inventory of Bibles that are in the classrooms. Many churches (especially older ones) have a variety of Bibles that have been there for years in closets and on shelves in the classrooms. Many are very old and some are in poor condition.

Recently my husband and I were leading a workshop at a church when one of the teachers raised a question: "Why do we have such old Bibles in our classroom? They are falling apart. Besides, the children have a hard time reading them and everyone groans every time we get them out." We asked, "What version of the Bible are you using?" She answered, "I don't know." The church school superintendent said, "Maybe we should buy some new Bibles. Let's see what you are talking about." She went to a nearby cupboard and opened the door. The Bibles were piled in a haphazard way on the shelf. She opened one of the Bibles and said, "It is the King James Version." Someone asked, "What version do we give the children in the third grade?" The superintendent said, "We give them the *Good News Bible*." Then someone immediately chimed in, "That does not make sense. Why do we give the children one version as a gift and use another in the classroom?" Needless to say, the superintendents at this church are in the process of purchasing new Bibles for all the classes in the church school.

Many times we take things for granted or become so accustomed to the way things are that we forget to question if everything is as it should be. Check to see what Bibles are being used in your classrooms:

1. What translation is in the room?
2. Are there enough Bibles for the number of students who meet in each room?
3. Are all the Bibles the same or different editions?
4. What are the conditions of the Bibles?

While you are at it, look to see what study resource books are in the rooms. What did you find? Do the fifth and sixth grade classrooms have study helps available in the room? Are there atlases, concordances, dictionaries, and word books in sufficient number and in versions appropriate for the students?

The reason for asking if the Bibles are all the same edition is that it is much easier to teach when all the students are using the same edition. Having the same edition means that all the books are identical, with the same layout on every page and the same page numbers.

When we are introducing children to the Bible it is helpful if we can refer to page numbers to help students find references. It is desirable for everyone to find the same Bible helps, the same chapter and section headings, and the same illustrations when studying a passage.

While junior and senior high students and adults may benefit from having available a variety of translations when doing Bible study, there are still times when it is helpful, and sometimes necessary, for everyone to have the same translation. Look carefully to see that the resources in each room are appropriate for the students meeting in that room.

INTEGRATING BIBLE SKILLS
WITH CURRICULUM

———————

One thing that has become very clear to me is that for students to learn what we are trying to teach, there must be both repetition and relevance to the student's experience. In order to learn a Bible skill, it is absolutely necessary to use that skill over and over for an extended period of time until it becomes a natural response instead of something that has to be thought about each time it is used. The teacher may want to spend a Sunday or two introducing and working on a particular skill. This will be done with the intention of using it throughout the year along with the curriculum, because the teacher realizes that the way to effectively teach the skill is to provide the opportunity for the students to use it in purposeful ways.

It is one thing to learn how to do something just to learn how to do it. It is quite another thing to learn how to do something because you need that skill in order to do something else. If we teach Bible skills in September with the idea that the students will have them for the rest of their lives, whenever they happen to need them, we may be disappointed when a lesson comes along in March that requires the students to use the skills taught in September (but not used since) and they don't remember what to do. We remember how to do a skill because we have used it often to accomplish tasks that are important to us.

At the beginning of the year, the teacher needs to ask several important questions:

—**Which skills are appropriate for my class this year?**
—**What is an appropriate time to introduce each new skill?**
—**What activities can I use initially to teach the skill?**
—**Where, in my lesson plans, can I have the students use the skill?**
—**How can I reinforce the learning and use of the skill during the year?**

It is *very important* for the teacher to know what skills are being taught and used in school in order to know which Bible skills are appropriate for a particular class. If we know what skills are being worked on in school in reading, science, math, language arts, and social studies, we can make a good judgment about the ability of our students to use particular Bible skills. We can also be alert to the expectations of our curriculum. Most of the time curriculum writers do a good job, but occasionally they miss the mark. Sometimes first graders are expected to be able to use writing skills they do not have, or reading abilities that are still beyond them. Sometimes maps are introduced before children have developed their map skills sufficiently. Sometimes church school curriculum assumes students have abilities that have not been developed sufficiently to accomplish those things we are asking them to do. This is when children become discouraged, don't complete the work we have given them, or become disruptive in class. It is to our advantage, as well as to the students' advantage, for us to be alert to the abilities of our particular children. As we teach, we will discover that there is a great variance in ability from one group of children to another, from one individual to another, from one school district to another, and from one part of

23

the country to another. For this reason, I know that you, the reader, may disagree with some of my statements regarding abilities at various grade levels. You may read a statement about third graders and think to yourself—"but my children *can* do that." And you may be right! In the end, it is your responsibility to make decisions based on your observations of students. There is no way that I can know your children or your situation sufficiently to say that a particular activity is or is not appropriate for your class. The labels I am using come from my experiences of teaching a number of children and reflect what I have found to be true in my teaching.

It is good to avoid being so eager to teach the Bible that we rush children into something for which they are not ready. Most church school teachers are not professionally trained as teachers. Many do not have the skills required to introduce children to dictionary skills, alphabetizing skills, categorizing skills, or sequencing. It is best for the school teachers to teach these and for the church school teacher to build upon them after they have been mastered.

How does the church school teacher know what abilities the children have, or what skills are being taught in school? One way is to find the school teachers in the church and to talk to them. Another is to make contact with someone who teaches the same grade level in school that you teach in church and to make arrangements to visit the class occasionally during the year to observe the children and the teacher. If time is available and the opportunity is there, a wonderful experience is to become a teacher's aide for a period of time so that you can become involved with the students at school and observe a trained teacher in action.

If children need a great deal of help, ask many questions, and struggle trying to do the task assigned to them, these are signs that a skill is being introduced that is new or too difficult. When a teacher finds that something has been introduced too soon, I recommend that the teacher back off and drop the matter until later in the year. There is no reason why the teacher cannot stop in the middle of an activity and say, "This activity is not working out very well; let's do something else."

When looking for places in the curriculum to use Bible skills, the teacher needs to be alert to the activities the curriculum is suggesting and how these can be adapted so that the students have the opportunity to use Bible skills. For example:

> —*Perhaps the lesson encourages the comparison of the stories of the Resurrection in several Gospels. If so, students could be encouraged to use the cross-reference notes to find all the stories.*

> —*Maybe a lesson suggests that the theme is repeated in some other parts of the Bible. A concordance would enable students to follow up on finding other passages of scripture related to the theme of the lesson.*

> —*Some curriculums list the key words for each lesson. Whether listed or not, most lessons do have key words. Instead of the teacher simply defining the words, students could be given the task of using a Bible dictionary to look up the key words and to share the definitions and explanations with the rest of the class.*

> —*Whenever children have questions about customs, traditions, people of the Bible, or places in the Bible, the teacher can guide the children in the exploration of the questions by using reference books instead of the teacher's becoming the only source of answers to questions.*

These activities may not be suggested in the curriculum, but the teacher who is alert to opportunities to enrich the lesson and to provide ways for the students to use their Bible skills will find ways to adjust the suggested activities in order to accomplish these goals.

INTEGRATING BIBLE WITH SKILLS WITH CURRICULUM

Teachers should keep in mind that they cannot and should not try to teach all Bible skills in their class in one year. When we look at the development of our students' abilities, we realize that the teaching of Bible skills needs to be spread out over a long period of time. Skills can be taught in stages, one level of understanding at a time. It is a reality that students are beginning in the church school program at all grade levels. We cannot assume that all the children in a particular class have been in church school from grade one and have all been taught the same things. Our classes are composed of children who have had church school experience and know many stories and facts about the church, as well as children who have had very little exposure to church school. This makes teaching in the church a challenge and a very big responsibility. It means that every year, at every grade level, the teacher must assess the abilities and background of each student and mold the teachings for that year to fit that particular class.

The curriculum has a great deal to do with how much we do with Bible skills in a year. Some quarters of curriculum lend themselves more easily than others to integrating Bible skills which we have identified as goals for our class. A curriculum which places more emphasis on the content and structure of the Bible will facilitate the teaching of Bible skills to a greater extent than a curriculum which features contemporay issues, interpersonal relationships or feelings.

It would be to the church's advantage if the Christian education committee, or whatever group of people is responsible for the education of children in your church, took the time to write a set of objectives related to Bible skills for each grade level, based on the curriculum that is being used. Such a list of objectives would enable teachers of each grade level to know what skills their children should have mastered by the time they leave that grade level. This task would make the committee aware of the needs the teachers might have regarding help to accomplish the objectives. Supplementary materials for the curriculum may need to be developed. Help may be needed in planning sessions to adapt activities suggested by the curriculum so that the teaching of skills can be accomplished. In the next chapter, we will see some guidelines for matching Bible skills with the student's abilities and a variety of teaching activities that can be used to supplement those suggested by the curriculum.

IDENTIFYING STUDENTS' ABILITIES

Before we choose activities, it is good to look at some of the Bible skills we want to teach to see what abilities the children need in order to be successful. When looking at this list, keep in mind that each class will have some students working at grade level, some who are above grade level, and some who are below grade level. Some students will learn very quickly; others may take all year to become proficient. Church school teachers will need to be aware of each student's abilities as they change throughout the year.

Use the following chart as a guide to help you begin to evaluate and choose appropriate activities for your class. *The grade level on the chart reflects the average time when students have become proficient enough with a skill taught in school that they can use the skill by themselves, with little or no help from the teacher.* Many of the skills taught in school that are listed on the chart will be introduced to the children several years before the grade level indicated on the chart. In each skill area, there are several levels of learning. I am trying to suggest, through this chart, that we wait until the student has some proficiency before we ask the student to use it when we introduce a Bible skill. The chart may cause you to begin to look at Bible skills in a different way; consequently, it may cause you to develop different criteria for deciding what skills should be taught and when. If you drastically disagree with something on the chart, that is a signal that alerts you to double-check your information and to clarify for yourself the reasons for your decisions. When you are satisfied with the criteria you have developed for choosing activities for your class, proceed to the planning for your class.

When we look at the chart, we see that the third or fourth grade levels may be the most appropriate times to introduce Bible skills, but we must remember that in each of the above Bible skills there are several levels of learning that enable younger children to gain partial understanding of the skill. In one sense we start teaching Bible skills as soon as the child enters the church. Let me try to explain what I mean by describing activities we might do with non-readers and with beginning readers.

Before first grade

A child who encounters teachers and parents who read or tell stories from the Bible and hold the Bible open on their laps while doing so acquires the first skills of identifying the Bible as a special book about Jesus and God. This is the first step in discovering the Bible.

I used to take the above for granted. It seemed that the children I encountered in church school came to me knowing that the Bible was special and knowing that it was about God and Jesus. Recently I was reminded that this was something we should not take for granted when I listened to a teacher share one of her experiences.

One day this sixth grade teacher gave the assignment to look up something in the Bible. She noticed that two boys (one of whom was a visitor) were huddled over the Bible, frantically looking for the passage. She went over to see if she could be of some help. As she talked to the boys, she

Identifying Abilities Needed for Bible Skills

BIBLE SKILLS	ABILITIES NEEDED	GRADE MOST STUDENTS CAN USE THE SKILL INDEPENDENTLY
Understanding how the Bible came to be	Sense of history and chronology	5-6
Understanding the difference between Old Testament and New Testament	Sense of time and history	3-4
Finding books, chapters, and verses; using cross reference notes	Reading, alphabetizing, use of numerical order	3-4
Learning abbreviations of the names of the books of the Bible	It helps to know how to abbreviate, but some students can memorize and use without understanding why we use these letters	3-4
How to use a concordance, a dictionary and a word list	Dictionary skills, alphabetical order, use of guide words, and sequencing	4
Using maps	Global concept of space and direction. Understanding of political and natural boundaries and differences between cities, states, countries, empires	5
Categorizing books of the Bible into proper sections: Gospels, Psalms, Letters, Law, History, Prophets, etc.	Ability to categorize. Understanding and identifying different types of literature	5-6
Using footnotes	Advanced reading skills. Understanding what footnotes are, and how to use them	Youth

found out that the visitor, who had come just to be with his friend, had not had any experience with the Bible before that day. He had not seen one before and did not know anything about it. What a challenge! As I listened to this account, I realized that recognition of the Bible as a special book about Jesus and God is indeed basic, so we start working on it when children are very young—and we must never stop working on it.

Another skill that can be learned at this age is that the Bible has two parts called the Old Testament and the New Testament. The child should not be expected to fully understand the differences between them, but the teacher who uses the words *Old Testament* and *New Testament* when talking about where the stories come from may instill in these young children the knowledge that there are two parts to the Bible.

First grade

In the first grade, we are more intentional in our teaching about the differences between the Old and the New Testaments, and we reinforce the concept that the Bible is a special book which tells us about God and Jesus and our relationship with them. We will also teach that the Bible is like a library which has many books in it. We will not necessarily teach the names of the books, nor will we be concerned about the children's finding certain books in the Bible.

The teacher may open the Bible to the story which is going to be told. As an introduction to the story, the teacher might say, "The story we are going to hear today is from the New Testament. The name of the New Testament book where we find this story is _____. Or the teacher might say something like, "The story I am going to tell you today happened a long time ago before Jesus was born. The story is from the Old Testament." If the children hear such phrases enough times, eventually they will remember that there are two parts to the Bible and that the Old Testament contains stories about things that happened before Jesus was born, and the New Testament contains stories about Jesus' life and the early church.

The teacher may also spend some time showing the children the Bible. Open the Bible to the beginning of the New Testament. Look at how thick the Old Testament is compared to the New Testament. Look at the illustrations in each testament and talk about the kinds of stories that are in each.

After the beginning of the new year, sometime in February, the first grade teacher will see a marked difference in the reading abilities of the children. Many of the children will be reading very well. When the teacher notices this, it is appropriate to begin printing short verses on the chalkboard or a newsprint chart for the children to read aloud. Printing the name of the book of the Bible before telling the story, or printing the names of the people in the story for the children to see, will also help to develop recognition skills that are basic to learning future skills. To do this, the teacher needs to develop the skill of printing. Practice your printing. If this is a new skill for you, find some paper and a chart at a school supply store, or go to a first grade teacher in a near-by public school and ask for help. It is especially helpful to the children if you use the same style of printing that is being used in their schools. In fact, if you use another style, the children are likely to tell you that you are not doing it right, and some children may have difficulty reading what you are printing.

Near the end of the year, if you are teaching stories from the Gospels, you might teach the children the names of the four Gospels and explain what the word *gospel* means. To practice learning the names of the Gospels and the order in which they appear in the Bible, you could make up a simple set of four large cards that can be used as flash cards, or mixed up on a table and placed in order several times. Another way to practice the order is to make a chart with four boxes in a row and let the children place the cards in the right spaces.

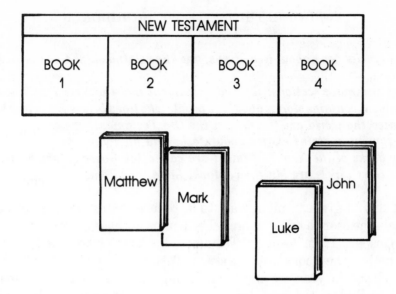

The four cards could be dislayed on a bulletin board. When the teacher is ready to tell a story, the children are told which book the story is from. A volunteer may be given the privilege of going to the bulletin board and finding the correct card to place with a picture that illustrates the story.

Remember that to use these cards in any way requires that the students be able to read the names of these four books. The teacher will decide whether or not this activity is appropriate by determining how many students can read the names of the books. If most of the students will not be successful with the activity and some will, the teacher may decide to wait and use the activity in the second grade when more of the students will be ready for it. If the teacher decides to go ahead and use the activity anyway, the children in the class who have not developed their reading abilities should be given other tasks that they can succeed at so that they do not feel put on the spot or inferior. Even in the second grade, there may be some students whose reading ability has not developed sufficiently for them to be successful with this activity.

Second grade

The reading abilities of second-graders may differ a great deal from child to child. For most second-graders, reading is an exciting new skill. Many of them want to read everything in sight. As the teacher opens the Bible to tell a story from it, second-graders (and sometimes first-graders) will want to see the words in order to try reading them. Even though there will be some second-graders who can, indeed, read most of the words in a Bible story, remember that reading does not equal comprehension! It is still best for the teacher to tell or to read the story. Reinforce the enthusiasm for reading by giving opportunities to read selected verses that have been printed on the board (so other children can see the words and read them, too) or make available some children's storybooks that have a simple vocabulary and that present the same story the teacher has told from the Bible. These storybooks can be made available for the children to read on their own, or a teacher may sit with a small group gathered around to read the story and to look at the pictures together. The reading of the book may be shared by the teacher and several of the students. Time can be spent looking at pictures, learning difficult words, and talking about the story as it is read.

Teachers of second-graders will want to reinforce the understanding that:

—The Bible is a special book about God, Jesus, and the relationships God and Jesus have had with people.
—The Bible has two main sections: the Old Testament and the New Testament.
The Old Testament contains stories about the people who lived before Jesus was born. Stories about how God created the world are the first in the Old Testament.
—The New Testament contains stories about Jesus and his followers.
—The first four books of the New Testament are called the Gospels, which means "good news."
—The names of the Gospels are Matthew, Mark, Luke, and John.

The teacher of second-graders might want to introduce the names of some other books of the Bible which contain the stories being taught. The names of these books can be approached in the same way as the Gospels. If names of Old Testament books are introduced, we can begin to work on identifying whether the books are in the Old Testament or the New Testament.

Toward the middle of the year, we may begin giving out Bibles with a bookmark placed so that children can open the Bible to the page where the passage the teacher will be using as the basis for the day's story or for devotions is located. Children will enjoy doing some of the reading directly from the Bible when verses are carefully selected.

Allowing the children to hold an open Bible and see the words of the story the teacher has just told helps to increase the child's reverence for, interest in, and curiosity about the Bible. I'll never forget the excitement of one of my students when she discovered that the story I had just told the class was really in the Bible and she could read it. Her face lit up like a light. She jumped up from her seat and called to me with an excited voice, "Mrs. Griggs, Mrs. Griggs, the story is right here; it's really in the Bible, and I can read it!"

We need to be careful about which stories and passages we expect the children to be able to read. Look first to see how many new words will need to be defined. Look to see what concepts may be difficult to understand. Identify what needs to be cleared up before the children are given the passage to read. You can work on difficult words and definitions before encountering them in the story. Work on difficult concepts so that when they are encountered in the story attention is not diverted from the story as the concept is struggled with.

If a student is given the responsibility of reading aloud, be sure the groundwork has been done ahead of time to enable a smooth reading. Those who are listening can easily lose interest and become impatient if the person reading aloud stumbles on words, needs help with many words, or generally cannot read the passage with meaning.

I advocate the telling of the story by the teacher first. After the story is familiar and there is some understanding of it, the opportunity may be given for the children to become involved with reading the scriptures.

The foundations are being laid so that when the children reach the latter half of the third grade, or enter the fourth grade, they will be able to build on what they already know as they learn new skills.

Another example of seeing levels of understanding in one skill is to look at the skill of putting books of the Bible into their proper categories. Suppose a third grade teacher is working on the stories of Moses. This teacher is calling attention to the books of Exodus, Numbers, and Deuteronomy as various parts of the story is presented. By the end of the stories of Moses the teacher has, with very little effort, introduced several books belonging together in one section of the Bible. With a little more attention and time, the teacher could talk about the Torah and help the children to learn the names of the other two books that belong with those that have already been introduced.

Perhaps a class is working on a psalm. Second and third-graders know what a poem is and what a song is. Identifying the psalm as poetry would be a natural thing to do. The same holds true for law, history, and letters. If the children become familiar with the type of literature they are studying at the time, when they reach the grade in which they are expected to work on the categories of the Bible (usually fifth or sixth grade) they will already have a foundation on which to build. Much will have been learned already. But to try and learn all the categories of the Bible and all the genres in each in the third grade would be an overwhelming and needlessly difficult task. It is better to be happy with teaching a little at a time and to wait until the student is older to put it all together as the structure of the Bible is studied.

With these examples of ways to look at the development of skills and with the chart to use as a guide, we are ready to start selecting activities.

ACTIVITIES FOR TEACHING BIBLE SKILLS

The following activities have been developed to go along with other teaching activities and experiences that you will provide for your students. Some of the activities are appropriate for introducing a skill. All of them are meant to reinforce the skill that is being worked on. By having worksheets, games, and puzzles available to them throughout the year, students have the opportunity to review and to practice as often as they need to.

When I developed the following activities, I found that it was helpful to create a box that I called the Activity Box, in which to store the materials for the activities so that they would be readily available to students when needed.

Most Sundays there was a game, puzzle, or other activity that was used in the class to reinforce the learning of a story or a Bible skill. When church school was over each Sunday, I would take copies of the activity sheet or the game(s) that were used and put them in a large manila envelope. The instructions for using the activity sheet or for playing the game were printed on the outside of the envelope. If there was no activity sheet or game related to the lesson for a Sunday, I often would go home and create something that would help a student become familiar with the story or skill we had worked on that day. This activity or game would be put into an envelope with instructions printed on the outside, and the envelope would be added to the Activity Box the next Sunday morning.

At Second Presbyterian Church, church school began when the first child arrived—around 9:15 A.M.—and ended about 10:40 A.M. Since I was reluctant to begin the new lesson before the majority of children were there (around 9:40), I encouraged the children to use the Activity Box for that first twenty to thirty minutes. Another choice of activity was to go to the book corner to find a book to look at, or to sit on the pillows with a teacher who would tell a story or read a book to the children.

The games which had game boards were placed next to the Activity Box. An instruction card was attached to each game board with a paper clip. Small boxes held timers, spinners, and playing pieces.

Fortunately, I taught with a team of teachers. The three of us divided ourselves among the children so that we could play with them, read with them, or help them with activity sheets.

I also used the Activity Box idea when I taught at St. Catherine's School. The box was very important in this situation because it was available to those children who finished assignments early or those who had missed a session and had to make it up. Since I had to give grades at St. Catherine's I had to find ways to evaluate the work and chart the progress of each student. I found that the reinforcement and review that were provided by the Activity Box were absolute necessities if students were to learn the material thoroughly. The message I have for church school teachers, based on my experiences at St. Catherine's, is: *Take your time when you are teaching. Don't hesitate to review and review again. Repetition is necessary for students to learn stories and skills. We must slow down and take our time.* Sometimes it is necessary to take more than one Sunday on a particular lesson for the material to be learned. The problem with this kind of teaching is that if we slow down and take our time to allow for repetition and reinforcement, we will not move through the curriculum as quickly as we would if we were faithful to the time-table the curriculum presents. It is hoped that the more leisurely pace will be supported by parents, by other teachers, and by the church staff.

The activities you will find on the following pages are for reinforcement. These activities need to be used in conjunction with other teaching activities for students to learn. It is so important for the Bible skills to be integrated into the regular curriculum, so that the students are able to have valid reasons for using the skills and to get the practice they need in order to master them. These activities cannot do the job alone. I hope they will be of help to you and that you will find excitement in this part of the experience of opening the Bible with your students.

As you look through these activities, keep in mind the abilities your students must have in order to do them. Choose only those activities that are appropriate and that will aid you in accomplishing your objectives. Perhaps some of the activities will stimulate your creativity so that you can use the activity as a springboard to create your own activity sheets and games. I hope this happens because the activity will then be created with your specific class in mind, and it will be more appropriate for them.

----

1. Involve the family in the child's exploration of the Bible. Send a worksheet for the student to fill in at home. Encourage the students to ask for help at home. The worksheets should be brought back to church school and the information shared and discussed. (A sample worksheet is presented on the following page.)

DEVELOPMENT OF THE BIBLE

The activities you choose to use in order to teach students about the development of the Bible will depend on the grade you are teaching, how much you want to develop the subject, and what resources you have available to use. Choose and adapt the following activities to fit your objectives and the resources you have available. Perhaps the following will suggest other activities that you can develop yourself and that will be more appropriate for your class.

2. Gather a number of translations of the Bible to bring to class. Students could be encouraged to bring Bibles from home. Hebrew and Greek Bibles can be borrowed from the pastor. Give the students time to look at all the different Bibles and to notice how they are alike and how they are different. Make a list of questions that are raised as students look at the different Bibles. Use these questions as a basis for outlining future lessons, or take time to explore as many of the questions as you have time for during this session.

Have available information from the American Bible Society about the work they do in the translating of the scriptures. They have very interesting information which they will send to you (American Bible Society, P.O. Box 5601, Grand Central Station, New York, NY 10163).

3. Invite the pastor to your class to tell the students about his or her experiences in learning Greek and Hebrew in seminary and how learning these languages is important for the Bible study that is done in preparation for preaching and teaching in the church. Perhaps the pastor will teach the students a few Hebrew or Greek letters or words and show the students the Hebrew or Greek Bible as he or she tells about it.

(Sample worksheet)

Exploring Bibles at Home*

Name_____

1. Find the following words in a dictionary (or a Bible dictionary if you have one). Write down the meanings of the words.

Bible_____

_____

Testament   (If you cannot find the word Testament, look for Testimony.)

_____

_____

Gospel _____

What are some reasons you think the first four books of the New Testament are called Gospels?

_____

_____

2. What *versions* of the Bible do you have at home? (The name of the version will appear on the title page of the Bible.)_____

_____

3. Does your family have a *family Bible?* If so, what are some things you discover about this Bible that makes it different from other Bibles?_____

_____

_____

4. Sometime this week talk with your family about why the Bible is an important book to study. Write a paragraph or more to share what you have found out.

*Worksheet to be sent home with students.

---

4. Find out if there are any students in your class who can speak a language other than English. If so, ask them to say something in that language. Ask if anyone who does not know that language could understand what was being said. Have the student translate what was said into English. If none of the students speaks another language, invite someone from the congregation to come in and teach the students several words or phrases to demonstrate the process of translation. Perhaps someone could share his or her experiences of learning a new language or trying to communicate with someone who does not understand.

5. Play a game of charades using familiar Bible passages. To play charades, you need two or more teams. Write the Bible passages, or Bible story episodes, on slips of paper (the whole passage—not just the reference). A representative from one team draws a slip of paper from a bowl, reads it silently, and shows the paper to the other team if desired. The task of the student who drew the slip of paper is to communicate to his or her own team what is written on the paper without using any words. It is best to use verses, or story episodes, with which all the students are familiar. Use a timer of some sort so that there will be a limit for each turn. Score is kept by keeping track of the amount of time each team takes to correctly guess the verse. At the end of the game, whichever team has the least amount of time wins.

6. See a filmstrip about the Dead Sea Scrolls, or share books about the Dead Sea Scrolls which have pictures of the Qumram community, the jars in which the scrolls were found, the scrolls and fragments, and so forth. Explore the subject of scrolls. How were the first ones made? How were they preserved? How were they used? What have the discoveries of ancient scrolls taught us about the development of our Bible? (A few books and a filmstrip that would help you with this are listed in the bibliography.)

7. Make some simple scrolls.
1. Provide a long, narrow piece of paper for each student.
2. Provide two small dowels that are a little longer than the paper is wide.
3. If students have learned to look up verses or are in the process of learning how, give them a verse to locate in the Bible and to copy onto their scrolls.

Directions for the students.
a. Put your name on one side of the paper.
b. Turn the paper over.
c. Look up this reference—Deuteronomy 6:4-8.

　　　　　　　　　　Book　Chapter　Verses

d. Read the verse.
e. Copy the verses carefully onto your paper. You may print in columns from left to right, or you may start at the right side of your paper and print in columns as the Hebrews did.
f. When you finish, tape the dowels to the ends of your paper by following these steps:
　Place the tape sticky side up on the table.
　Lay the paper on half of the sticky tape.
　Lay the dowel on the other half of the sticky tape.
　Press down. Roll the dowels to the middle of the paper.

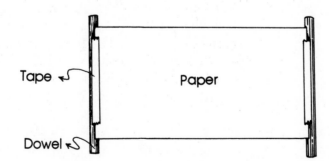

8. Take a field trip to a synagogue. The pastor of your church may know one of the rabbis in town and may be able to make the contact for you. Be sure to talk to the rabbi, or whoever will be your host or hostess for the visit, to help that person understand why you want to bring the children and what you want them to experience. The more information you can provide, the more likely you are to have the kind of experience you are hoping for. The children are usually very impressed with such a visit and are fascinated by the Ark, the coverings on the scrolls, the size of the scrolls, the history of the scrolls being used in the particular synagogue, and all that the rabbi tells them about the way the scrolls are used in worship.

9. Create some crossword puzzles to reinforce the learnings about the development of the Bible. To develop a crossword puzzle, follow these few simple steps:

a. Decide on the subject you want to be the focus. The younger the student, the more focused the subject should be and the fewer words used. Some sample subjects could be: Overview of the Development of the Bible, People, Places and Events, Scrolls, and so on.
b. Make up a list of the words that you want to include in your puzzle.
c. Start with one word, perhaps the longest, in a horizontal or vertical position somewhere near the center of the page.
d. It is helpful to use graph paper in developing your puzzle.
e. Use a pencil so you can erase easily. Try words in various places. Be sure to erase a word when it does not fit where you put it. Work with the words until all are included. Don't worry about the form or the shape of the puzzle design.
f. Use a clean piece of paper to trace the spaces of the completed puzzle.
g. Start at the top left-hand corner of your puzzle and number all your words from left to right.
h. Make up a set of clues related to the words of the puzzle. Put the number of the word next to the clue that matches it.
i. Duplicate the puzzle for the students.
j. Make up a copy or two of the completed puzzle to have as an answer sheet in the classroom, or you could simply have a list of the answers available.

Following is a sample puzzle and answer sheet.

Clues across:

1. A book of songs and poems found in the middle of the Bible.
4. The first book in the New Testament: the name of one of Jesus' disciples.
5. The language in which the Old Testament was written.
7. The _____ Testament contains stories about Jesus and the early church: has twenty-seven books.
8. Christians believe it contains the *word of God.*
10. The Dead Sea Scrolls were hidden in _____ pots.
11. The books of Matthew, Mark, Luke, and John are called _____.
14. Early scrolls were made of _____.
15. The community of scribes and other religious people who lived near the Dead Sea and preserved many scrolls.
16. The Dead _____ was called *dead* because no creatures could live in it.
17. The _____ Testament contains thirty-nine books and includes stories about Abraham, Moses, David, and many other kings and prophets.
18. Means beginning; the first book of the Bible.

Clues down:

2. Title of a person who copied the Bible from one scroll to another.
3. Scrolls are also _____ which means *written by hand*.
6. The Bible is often called the _____ of God.
9. The Bible is divided into _____, there are sixty-nine of them.
12. The Qumram community copied them.
13. The New Testament was first written in_____.

	ACROSS		DOWN
1.	Psalms	11. Gospels	2. Scribe
4.	Matthew	14. Papyrus	3. Manuscripts
5.	Hebrew	15. Qumram	6. Word
7.	New	16. Sea	9. Books
8.	Bible	17. Old	12. Scrolls
10.	Clay	18. Genesis	13. Greek

10. Create your own game, using a format similar to the popular game Trivial Pursuit, related to information the children have been discovering in their studies. The most effective way to use this game is to have the students create the questions and the answers. They will learn a great deal about the subject if they are responsible for the information on the cards.

1. Have the students work in teams of two or three.
2. Provide enough resources for the students to find information and to do research.

3. Each team is given (or chooses) one area or category of the subject to work on. For example:

a. Scrolls
b. Translations
c. People

d. History
e. Organization of the Bible

4. Students create a list of questions and answers. The list is shown to the teacher. The teacher may want to make suggestions that will clarify the questions and answers or to improve the quality of the questions.
5. During the week, find someone to type up the cards.
   —Use 3″ × 5″ cards.
   —Use a different color of card for each category of questions.
   —Type the question on one side of the card and the answer on the other.
6. Play the game in class.

If the class is large, it might be a good idea to have several sets of cards so that several games can be going on at the same time.

Preparing to play the game:
1. Use a spinner that has the numbers 1 through 5 (or numbers that correspond to the categories of questions that have been developed).
2. Give each category of questions a number. Each category already has a different color associated with it because you have used various colors of cards on which to type the questions. Using a colored marking pen, circle the number on the spinner with the color of the category it represents.

For example:

Scrolls	(yellow)	#1
Translations	(pink)	#2
Key People	(blue)	#3
History	(green)	#4
Organization of the Bible	(buff)	#5

3. Take some blank 3″ × 5″ cards, or some construction paper that is the same color as the cards used for the questions, and cut them into one-inch squares. These will be used for keeping score.
4. Take more blank 3″ × 5″ cards and cut them into symbol shapes. Have one symbol for each category. Make several copies of each symbol.

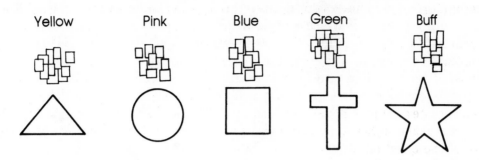

5. Prepare a playing surface on which to place the question cards, the score cards (one-inch squares), and the symbol cards. This playing surface may be made out of poster board, heavy butcher paper, or some other durable paper.

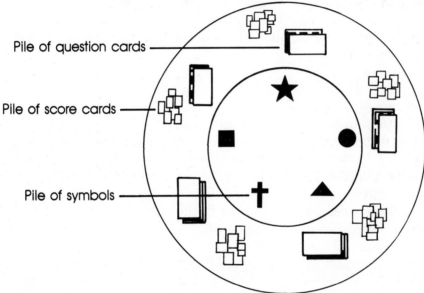

To play the game:
1. Player spins. When the arrow stops, another player draws a card from the pile that corresponds to the number and to the color on which the arrow stopped. This person reads the question to the player, making sure the answer is covered.
2. If the player answers the question correctly, the player earns one score piece from that category and another turn.
3. If the player does not answer the question correctly, the card is simply returned to the bottom of the pile from which it was taken.
4. All cards are returned to the bottom of their piles after a player has responded—whether correctly or incorrectly.
5. If a player earns five score pieces from one category, the five pieces are traded for a symbol card of that category.
6. If a player spins and lands on a category for which a symbol card has been earned, one more spin is allowed to try and land on another category. If unsuccessful, the turn is lost until the next time.
7. To win, a player must have one symbol card from each of the categories.

11. Create and play a game modeled after the familiar game Concentration. The game is played with a set of cards which is made of pairs of matching cards. The cards are mixed up and placed facedown on a table or on the floor. The object of the game is to find the pairs of cards that match. The person who finds the most pairs wins.

To make a set of concentration cards, blank playing cards may be used, or 3″ × 5″ cards cut in half may be used. Most school supply stores carry sets of blank playing cards which work very well.

To prepare your game:
1. Cut 3″ × 5″ cards in half so they are 2½″ × 3″ or use blank playing cards.
2. Use a permanent ink pen or any writing instrument that will not rub off or smear the cards.
3. Find a container for your cards. I like to use a medium-sized manila envelope. These envelopes are sturdy and will take a lot of wear. They are also large enough so that I can print the instructions for playing the game on the outside.
4. Place the directions on the envelope or on a separate piece of paper inside.
5. Make up an answer sheet and place it inside the envelope.
6. Place the cards inside the envelope and make the game available to your students.

Sample directions for the students
1. Mix up the cards and place them facedown on a table or on the floor.
2. First player turns over any card.
3. Read the card, then turn over another card that you think will relate.
4. If the two cards match, you may remove them and put them in front of you. Take another turn.
5. If the two cards do not match, turn the cards over again so they are facedown.
6. The next player follows the same rules.
7. The player with the most correct matches at the end of the game wins.
8. Use the answer sheet to check the answers.

Decide on the combination of words that you want to use. Learning takes place more quickly if we limit the number of cards included in the game. I like to use no more than twelve cards per set. Following is a sample set of cards for reinforcing some facts about the Bible:

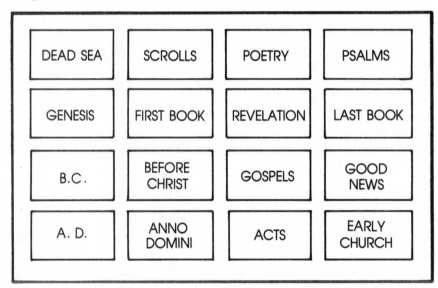

ABBREVIATIONS

Learning abbreviations is important if a student is going to use footnotes, cross-references, dictionaries, or concordance study helps. Most Bibles have a listing in the front that tells what the abbreviations for the various books are. The extent to which abbreviations are used varies with the Bible translation. Look to see how they are used in the version your students are using.

Some teachers prefer to teach the abbreviation for the name of a book when they introduce that book. Some prefer to wait until the students are in the fouth or fifth grades to begin using abbreviations. Other teachers do not teach abbreviations until students begin to use cross-references, footnotes, dictionaries, and concordances in the fifth or sixth grades.

When students are first learning about their Bibles and how to look up references, I think it is a good idea to print the complete name of a book when putting references on a chart, on a chalkboard, or in a worksheet. After the students have learned the name of the book (can recognize it, read it, pronounce it, spell it, and write it), they are ready to learn to abbreviate it.

Matching games are helpful ways to reinforce the learning of abbreviations. These games are like self-tests. The students discover from playing the games which abbreviations are familiar and which are not. Playing the games eventually helps students to remember the abbreviations.

Teach the abbreviations as you are studying the books—a few at a time. The best way to learn them is to incorporate them into the activities of a lesson. Students who have been absent, or those who are having trouble remembering abbreviations well enough to comfortably complete activities during the lesson, can be helped by playing matching games and other reinforcement activities.

12. Instructions for creating a game like Concentration were given in the last section. When creating concentration games for abbreviations, decide which books of the Bible you will include in the game. You will probably want to include the books that will be studied during the year you have the children in your class. Learning takes place more quickly if fewer books are used in each game. Include no more than eight books in one game. If the cards are going to be used by individuals playing alone instead of in groups, more success will be experienced if four or five books per game are used. If you want to teach more books than the number suggested, it would be good to make up several sets of cards using a different color of card (or different color of ink) for each set. This will work better than putting the names of all the books in one game.

(Sample answer sheet for one set of cards)			
John	Jn	Mark	Mk
Luke	Lk	Psalms	Ps
Acts	Ac	Matthew	Mt
Genesis	Gn	Exodus	Ex

FINDING REFERENCES

Unless you know what the punctuation in a reference means, you have difficulty understanding that reference. We often take for granted that the students know what a hypen, a colon, and a comma represent in Bible references. It is as important to understand what these symbols mean as it is to understand which numbers represent chapters and which ones verses. I have heard students ask many times, "Do I stop at verse six, or do I read all of verse six?"

It is not necessary to wait until these punctuations marks are learned in grammar lessons in school for us to use them in biblical references. Actually, the way the marks are used in biblical references may be a little different from their use in standard grammar. Because their use is simple and unique in biblical references, most children can learn them easily.

Even the word *reference* needs to be defined. It is true that many adults become so accustomed to the unique vocabulary used in Bible study that it is easy to forget that with children we are teaching new words and concepts as well as teaching about the faith. The following are simple statements which can be used to define the parts of a Bible reference.

Reference	The reference contains the name of the book, the number of the chapter, and the verse or verses that we want to find.
Colon	The colon separates the chapter number from the verse numbers.
Period	Sometimes a period is used instead of the colon.
Hyphen	A hyphen tells us to read all the verses. In the following reference, we would read all the verses from verse 2 to and *including* verse 5. *Matthew 18:2-5*
Comma	A comma tells us to read only the verses listed in the reference. In the following reference, we would read only verses 2 and 5. *Matthew 18:2, 5*
a, b	*a* means you read only the first part of the verse. *b* means you read only the second part of the verse.

13. Make up some punctuation mark signs that can be used on a bulletin board or propped on a chalk rail. The signs could be made from tag board or construction paper. The students may enjoy making the signs themselves. The idea is to use the cards whenever you are working with a Bible reference so that the students become familiar with how to use the various punctuation marks in constructing a reference.

To make signs:

—Print the name of the book on a piece of tag board.

—Print one number on each piece of tag board until you have a sufficient number of signs or cards to make up a variety of Bible references.

—Make several signs that have a colon on them, several with commas, several with hyphens, several with *a* and several with *b*. If you are going to use a period instead of a colon, make up several signs with a period on them. You will decide which one to use by looking to see how references are presented in the Bibles the students are using and in the curriculum materials you are using. After the students have learned the use of the period or the colon, introduce them to the other symbol so that they feel comfortable with both ways of stating a reference.

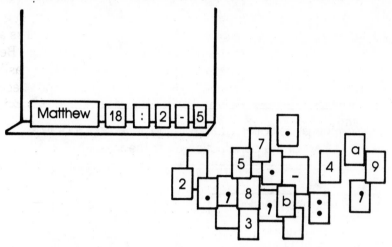

Use the signs:
- —Display the signs along the chalk rail, on a table, on a bulletin board, or somewhere that they can easily be seen by the students.
- —Arrange the signs to show the reference in the correct order.
- —The teacher can let the children arrange the signs by saying the reference aloud, then giving the students the chance to select the correct signs.
- —After creating the reference, students are encouraged to find the passage in their Bibles and then read it in unison.

14. The above signs (or cards) can be used on a bulletin board. Place all the signs in a box near the bulletin board. Have students select the signs that are needed for the reference and pin them on the bulletin board. A picture that illustrates the biblical passage might already be on the board which, when put with the reference, adds to the understanding of where the story or passage is found in the Bible.

15. Make a matching game by printing the statements about each punctuation mark on cards and the punctuation marks on other cards. Let the students put the cards on a bulletin board in two columns, showing which mark goes with each statement.

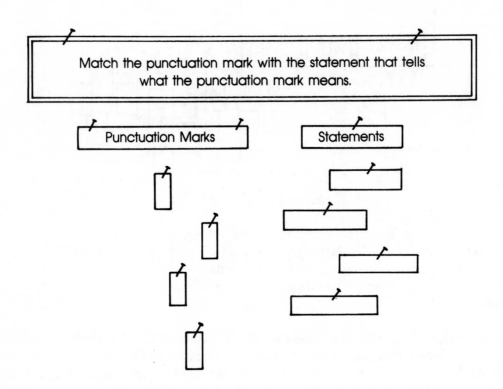

16. (Sample worksheet)

Meanings of Punctuation Marks

Draw a line from the punctuation mark to the statement that tells you what the punctuation mark does in the Bible reference.

b.   Means you only read the verses that go with the numbers in the reference.

—   Separates the chapter number from the verse number.

:   Tells you to read all the verses from the first verse to and including the last verse number.

,   Tells you to read the last part of the verse.

Complete the following:

The Bible reference contains the name of the _____,

the _____ number and the numbers of the _____

we need to find.

When beginning to work with punctuation marks to discover what their functions are in a reference, students need to use the punctuation marks in actual references to practice finding books, chapters, and verses, and to practice writing references. The following worksheet, created to be used with the *Good News Bible,* is one way to get this practice.

17. (Sample worksheet)

Finding Books, Chapters, and Verses

When you are trying to find a story or a verse in the Bible, you need to know:

Which book? Which chapter? Which verse?

If I wanted you to find a verse that appears in the New Testament in the book of John, I would write it this way.

John 3:16

First I put the name of the book..John
Then I put the number of the chapter...3
Then I put a colon after the chapter number... :
Then I put the number of the verse I want you to find.....................................16

See if you can find John 3:16.

1. Look in the table of contents to see what page the book of John starts on.

2. Find the book of John. The name of the book appears at the top of the page in larger print.

3. Find the chapter number. The chapter number is a large number on the page. It also appears at the top of the page in the corner with the name of the book.

4. Find the verse numbers. These will be small numbers. When you find the chapter number 3, look at the small numbers at the beginning of each verse. Find the number 16.

Read verse 16. Stop when you come to the number 17.

Write the words of verse 16 here:

_____

_____

---

18. A way to help students practice finding references and to get used to identifying where chapter numbers, verse numbers, and the name of the book appear on pages of the Bible is to duplicate a page from the version that your class uses. I have taken a page from the *Good News Bible* and enlarged it on the copy machine (see the enlargement on page 48). Enlarging makes it easier for beginning students to find verse numbers. After some practice, they will easily find the numbers in their Bibles. After making a number of copies, I put these pages in a manila envelope. The envelope is kept in the activity box for students to use whenever they have time to work on extra reinforcement activities. In choosing which page, or pages, to include in the envelope, I look for:

—A page that is laid out in an attractive way and has all the elements I want the students to find.

—A Bible reference that is appropriate for my students to read and become acquainted with. If they are going to work with a reference, it should be one that has a message for them. Often I choose a passage from a story that we have just studied.

—It is an added benefit to have an illustration that can be colored when the assignment is finished, but it is by no means a high priority.

Here are some instructions you could put on the envelope:

1. Take a page from the envelope.
2. What is the name of the book in the Bible that this page was taken from? Put a *rectangle* around the name of the book.
3. Find the numbers for the chapters on the page. Put a *circle* around the chapter numbers.
4. Find the numbers of the verses in chapter 21. Put a *line* under the verse numbers. Start with verse 1 and stop at verse 6.
5. Can you find verse 8 in chapter 21? A reference that would lead you to find this verse would look like this:

Matthew 21:8

6. What does verse 8 say? Take a piece of paper and copy the words of verse 8.
7. When you finish working with your page, take it and the paper with the verse you copied to a teacher to share what you have done.

There are many times when we are directed to read one part of a verse and not the whole thing. The verse may be very long, or it may contain more than one thought. (Don't forget that chapters and verses were added when printers started setting the Bible in type so that it would be easier to find Bible references. The original Greek and Hebrew appeared as continual text with no numbers of chapters or verses.)

When we see a reference that contains a letter, such as Genesis 2:4b, we are being told to read only the second half of verse 4 in the second chapter of Genesis. Since these letters do not appear in the text of thh Bible, students often have a great deal of trouble understanding what part of the verse to read. It is often difficult for adults to make this judgment also. Unless such a reference appears in the curriculum materials that your students are using, I would refrain from teaching about *a* and *b* until sixth grade or later.

WORKING WITH BOOKS

When working at familiarizing the students with the names of the books of the Bible, it is good to work with a few books at a time. The most logical way to become acquainted with the names of books is to call attention to them as you engage students in the lessons week by week. When telling a story from the Bible, be sure to tell the students in which book the story may be found. Write the name of the book on the board. Have the students find the story in their Bibles after you have told following. ³⁰ Two blind men who were sitting by the road heard that Jesus was passing by, so they began to shout, "Son of David! Have mercy on us, sir!"

³¹ The crowd scolded them and told them to be quiet. But they shouted even more loudly, "Son of David! Have mercy on us, sir!"

³² Jesus stopped and called them. "What do you want me to do for you?" he asked them.

³³ "Sir," they answered, "we want you to give us our sight!"

³⁴ Jesus had pity on them and touched their eyes; at once they were able to see, and they followed him.

"God bless him who comes in the name of the Lord!" (21.9)

The Triumphant Entry into Jerusalem
(Mark 11.1-11; Luke 19.28-40; John 12.12-19)

21 As Jesus and his disciples approached Jerusalem, they came to Bethphage at the Mount of Olives. There Jesus sent two of the disciples on ahead ² with these instructions: "Go to the village there ahead of you, and at once you will find a donkey tied up with her colt beside her. Untie them and bring them to me. ³ And if anyone says anything, tell him, 'The Master needs them'; and then he will let them go at once."

⁴ This happened in order to make come true what the prophet had said:

⁵ "Tell the city of Zion,
   Look, your king is coming to
      you!
   He is humble and rides on a
      donkey
      and on a colt, the foal of a
         donkey."

⁶ So the disciples went and did what Jesus had told them to do: ⁷ they brought the donkey and the colt, threw their cloaks over them, and Jesus got on. ⁸ A large crowd of people spread their cloaks on the road while others cut branches from the trees and spread them on the road. ⁹ The crowds walking in front of Jesus and those walking behind began to shout, "Praise to David's Son! God bless him who comes in the name of the Lord! Praise be to God!"

¹⁰ When Jesus entered Jerusalem, the whole city was thrown into an uproar. "Who is he?" the people asked.

¹¹ "This is the prophet Jesus, from Nazareth in Galilee," the crowds answered.

Jesus Goes to the Temple
(Mark 11.15-19; Luke 19.45-48; John 2.13-22)

¹² Jesus went into the Temple and drove out all those who were buying and selling there. He overturned the tables of the moneychangers and the

ˢ The Master; *or* Their owner.
21.5 Zec 9.9.   **21.9** Ps 118.25-26.

19. A worksheet that helps students practice finding references, and at the same time reviews important information about the Bible and the placement of books, may look like this:

(Sample worksheet)

Exploring the Bible

The Bible is a collection of books, like a library. We can find books by using the table of contents. Do the following to practice using the table of contents.

1. Open your Bible to the table of contents. This page tells you the page number where each book begins. Notice that the books are divided into two groups. What is the name of each group of books?

   _____

   _____

2. How many books are in the Old Testament? _____
   How many books are in the New Testament? _____

3. What is the name of the:
   first book of the Bible? _____

   last book of the Bible? _____

   first book of the New Testament? _____

4. Look in the table of contents to find the following information. Fill in the page number and a check mark to show whether it is found in the Old or the New Testament.

Name of book	Page	Old Testament	New Testament
Psalms _____			
Deuteronomy _____			
Ruth _____			
Luke _____			
Amos _____			
Acts _____			
I Corinthians _____			
Isaiah _____			
2 Peter _____			

the story so that they can read it for themselves. Help students become acquainted with the placement of the books by making statements such as:

Our story is from the New Testament.
The story is from the book of Luke which is between Mark and John.
When you find the book of Luke, look for chapter 10.
Our story begins at verse 25. At the beginning of the story, there is a heading that says "The Parable of the Good Samaritan."

If we are careful to provide this kind of information whenever we expect students to look up passages (especially when they are first learning to do this), we are helping them not only to learn how to find references, but also to work on book identification and placement. After a while, when a number of stories from Luke have been read, the students will automatically know the order of Mark, Luke, and John, and they will know that these books are found in the New Testament.

A worksheet that helps students practice finding references, and at the same time reviews important information about the Bible and the placement of books, may look like this:

20. Use blank playing cards to make sets of cards with the names of the books with which you are working. These cards can be used along with the table of contents to:

1. Divide the cards into piles for Old Testament and New Testament.
2. Look through the cards to find the names of books that you recognize and can tell which testament they appear in. Use the table of contents to find out which testament the other books go in.
3. Put the cards in the correct order to show the sequence that the books appear in the Bible.

It is best to keep the number of cards in these sets manageable. Students can quickly become discouraged if all the books of the Bible are included in such a set of cards. If the cards are limited to those books which the class has been studying, students will have more success and will stick with the activity longer.

21. Make up some puzzles that, when put together, provide information about the Bible.

1. Use 4″×6″ cards, tag board or other sturdy material for your puzzles.
2. Using a writing instrument that does not run or smear, print the name of the book at the top.
3. Print information about that book on the rest of the card.
4. Cut a zig-zag line across the card to divide the puzzle into two pieces. (If you are doing this with older students, each puzzle could be divided into three or four pieces to make it more challenging.)
5. Make up puzzle cards for each of the books of the Bible that your class has been studying.
6. Mix all the puzzle pieces together and place them in a manila envelope.
7. Create a worksheet that has questions related to the information on the cards.
8. Duplicate the worksheet and put it in the envelope with the cards.

ACTIVITIES FOR TEACHING BIBLE SKILLS

Sample instructions for the outside of the envelope:

1. Take a set of cards and a worksheet from the envelope.
2. Put the puzzle together. You will have several cards when you finish. Each card will have the name of a book of the Bible and some information about that book.
3. When you finish putting the puzzle together, fill in the worksheet. The answers to the questions on the worksheet will be found by reading the information on the puzzle cards.

(Sample puzzle cards)

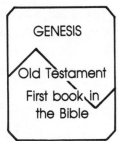

GENESIS — Old Testament — First book in the Bible

ACTS — New Testament — Stories about the early church

MARK — New Testament — Stories about Jesus; Second Gospel

DEUTERONOMY — Old Testament — A book of the Law

(Sample Worksheet)

Bible Book Puzzles

Put the puzzle pieces together. Read what the cards say. Look at the questions below and answer them according to the information on the puzzle cards.

1. Which books are from the Old Testament?
   _____
   _____

2. Which books are from the New Testament?
   _____
   _____

3. What are the names of the four Gospels?
   _____   _____
   _____   _____

4. Which book in the Bible is a book of poems?
   _____

5. The first book in the Bible is_____

6. The last book in the Bible is_____

7. God's laws for the Hebrews are found in the book of
   _____

8. We find the stories about people in the early church in the book of
   _____

22.

One way to work on pronunciation of the names of the books of the Bible and to help students become familiar with a variety of the books is to play Bible Book Bingo. This game can include as many of the books of the Bible as you want. You will want to include all the books that you know the class can recognize along with some that will be new to them. Perhaps the new books are the ones that will be introduced by the curriculum in the next unit or two of study.

1. Decide which books will be included in the game.
   Cut some pieces of heavy paper into pieces about one inch by two inches. On each piece, print the name of a book that you want to include in the game.

2. Each student will need a game card. I like to make several extra cards so that every student has a choice of game cards. A good size for these cards is about six inches by seven or eight inches.

   When making the game cards remember that:
   —not all cards will contain all the books included in the game.
   —the order that the books appear on the cards will be different for each card.

   When you make the game cards, work on the placement of books into either the Old or the New Testament by using a different color of ink for each. Or you can divide the cards into Old Testament columns and New Testament columns (see sample cards).

3. Students will need markers to cover the squares on their cards as the names of books are called. These can be small pieces of paper, beans or other small objects.

The game is played the same way as regular Bingo. Each student has a playing card and a number of markers. The teacher, or a student, can be the caller. A card is drawn from the pile and the name of the book is read aloud. Students look for the name of the book on their game cards and put a marker on it if they find it. The first player to cover five squares in a row calls "BINGO." You can vary the rules for the winning card, just as in regular Bingo. It is good for a teacher, or a helper, to join small groups that are playing the game to help with correct pronunciation of the names of the books.

(Sample Game Card)

Bible Book Bingo

Old Testament	Old Testament	Old Testament	New Testament	New Testament
Titus	Numbers	Genesis	Colossians	Mark
Psalms	Exodus	Esther	I John	Luke
Leviticus	Ruth	F R E E	James	Matthew
Isaiah	Joshua	Deuteronomy	Acts	Revelation
2 Kings	Daniel	Amos	I Timothy	Ephesians

The purposes of the game are to help students with pronunciation, familiarization with the names of the books, and with placeing books in the Old and New Testaments.

I like to store the game by putting each set of game pieces (game cards, playing pieces, and calling cards) into a different small envelope. All three of these small envelopes can then be put into a larger envelope with instructions for playing the game on the outside. This way everything for the game stays together. The instructions allow small groups of students to play the game on their own or for a whole class to play together.

TYPES OF LITERATURE AND BOOK PLACEMENT

There are several levels of learning for this subject. Students in the junior grades (third to fifth) may learn that Deuteronomy is a book of laws, that Psalms is a book of poetry, or that Mark is one of the four Gospels. As they have learned stories from these books, the teacher has called to attention the type of literature found in that book. But these students are not ready to work on identifying all the types of literature in the Bible or to deal with all the books of the Bible at once.

Students need to be familiar with a number of the books of the Bible and be able to recognize various types of literature before they can handle categorizing all the books of the Bible. If we do not wait for this development to take place, we are simply making students memorize for the sake of memorizing. Without constant use, this knowledge is often not retained. To include this skill before the sixth or seventh grade levels may be presenting a task that is too difficult for younger students. If we wait until sixth or seventh grade—or even later—to work with the entire Bible in this way, the students will have less difficulty because they will have learned in a gradual and purposeful way many of the books of the Bible, what kind of literature they represent, and where each book can be found in the Bible. There will be a foundation upon which to build. Older students will see the value of the skill and will be more motivated to learn.

When students have learned to categorize the books of the Bible, and when they are able to recognize the types of literature in each, they will discover that it is much easier to figure out where to look for particular books. They will know that Deuteronomy is a book of the law and must be in the front of the Old Testament. They will know that if they are looking for a book which is poetry, it will be found somewhere near the middle of the Bible. They will know that if the book they are looking for is a letter, it will be in the latter half of the New Testament.

Following are several reinforcement activities that may help students with this skill.

23. Make a bookshelf on which you can place small, individual-size cereal boxes that have been covered with self-adhesive paper. Write the name of a book of the Bible on the narrow side of the box. The boxes can be manipulated to show the correct order in which the books appear in the Bible and the categories to which the books belong. The shelf should be kept empty except for the books that the students are using. When the students become familiar with a book through their study of stories and passages of scripture from that book, the box is placed on the shelf. At the end of the year, the class can see how many books of the Bible they have explored. This activity can be used with younger students because we do not have to work with a large number of books. As the students become older, the activity can still be used because they will be familiar with more of the books and will become aware of types of literature and the placement of the book in the Bible.

There will be a time, when students are in junior high or older, that they will work with categorizing the books of the Bible in more depth. By this time, the skill will be easily learned by the children who have grown up in our church school because previous teachers have given attention to this subject. By the time children reach junior high, they realize that they have already learned a number of books and their placement, thus making the task easier.

A bookshelf could look something like this:

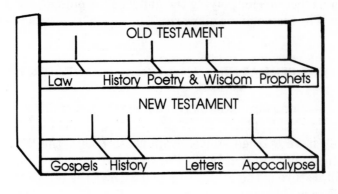

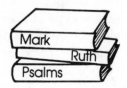

The shelf is labeled to show the Old Testament, the New Testament, and the categories of books that are contained in each testament. As students put the books on the shelf, they are placing them according to testament, to category, or to type of literature.

24. Make a chart that can be filled in as the books of the Bible are learned or as the class is working on the placement of the books in the Bible. Start with a blank chart. These can be individual charts, or you can have a large class chart. The chart can be added to at appropriate times during the year, or slips of paper with names of the books of the Bible can be attached to the chart when appropriate.

(Sample Chart)

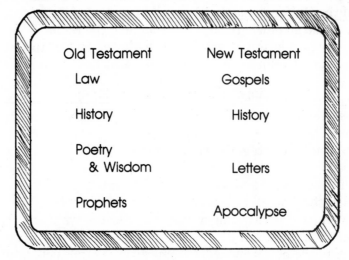

25. Another way to work with the names of the books of the Bible and with their placement in the Bible is to produce cards with the name of the book at the top and the name of its category, in another color of ink, below it.

1. Print the name of the Old Testament books in green ink.

2. Print the name of each New Testament book in blue ink.

3. Print the category that each book belongs in, using a different color of ink for each category.

   Categories you might include are:

Law	Poetry and Wisdom
History	Letters
Prophets	Gospels
Apocalypse	

To use the cards the students could:

1. Divide them into categories and work on one at a time to become familiar with the books in that category.

2. Use them as flash cards.

3. Make up a game to play with the cards that would help them learn the categories.

26. Create a Bible Book Categories Game.
First you need to make the cards for the game. On one side of the card, print the name of a book of the Bible. On the other side of the card, print the testament and the category in which it belongs.

For example:

Side One

Song
of
Songs

Side Two

Old
Testament
Poetry
and
Wisdom

Make several cards that say *TAKE ANOTHER TURN*. These will be mixed in with the other cards to add interest to the game.

You will need a spinner card. Blank spinner cards can be found at school supply stores. Divide the card so that you have one section for each category in the game.

Last, make a game board on which to play the game. I have included a sample game board which uses all the categories and has room for all the books in the Bible. Simpler game boards can be made if fewer categories are used and not all the books in the Bible are included in the game.

Put all the cards and the spinner in the envelope and the directions for playing the game on the outside of the envelope.

Directions for playing the game:

1. Shuffle the cards. All cards should have the side with the name of the book facing down.

2. Deal at least seven cards to each player. The number of cards that are dealt can vary with the number of players, but there should not be so many cards that they cannot be held easily in the hand. The game works best if there are four or more players.

3. Arrange the cards in your hand with the names of the books facing you. DO NOT look at the backs of the cards.

4. First player spins.

5. Place one card from your hand in a square on the game board that is in the category shown on the spinner. If you do not have a card for the category, you lose your turn.

6. If the spinner lands on TAKE A CARD, you must draw a card from the pile that is left over after dealing. Add it to your hand.

7. If you have a card in your hand that says TAKE ANOTHER TURN, lay it down, face up, in front of you. Any time during the game that you want to take another turn, you may use that card. You can use the card only once.

8. When the player has placed a card on the board, the other players may challenge the placement. If more than one player wants to challenge, take turns beginning with the challenger to the left of the player.
   —The challenger must name the category into which the card should be placed.
   —After the challenger names the category, check the placement of the card by looking at the back of the card.
   —If the player has placed the card in the right category, the challenger must draw a card from the pile of cards left after the deal, and add the card to his or her own hand.
   —If the player was wrong and the challenger was right, the card is moved to the correct category and the player must draw a card from the challenger's hand to add to his or her own hand.
   —If both the challenger and the player are wrong, both must draw a card from the pile.
   —If no one challenges the placement of a card, the player must still check the placement by looking at the back of the card. If the player put the card in the wrong category, it must be returned to the player's hand.

9. Take turns repeating the above steps.

10. The game ends when one person runs out of cards.

CROSS-REFERENCE NOTES

Many Bibles include cross-reference notes either beneath the title of a heading, at the bottom of the page, or in the margin. These notes help you to locate where the passage of scripture appears in other parts of the Bible. Students will be ready to learn how to use cross-reference notes after having become comfortable and competent at looking up Bible references. If we wait until students reach this stage in their abilities, and until using cross-references is an important part of their studying, it will be an easy skill to teach. Most curriculum resources will not indicate the use of cross-references until after grade five.

(Bible Book Categories Game)

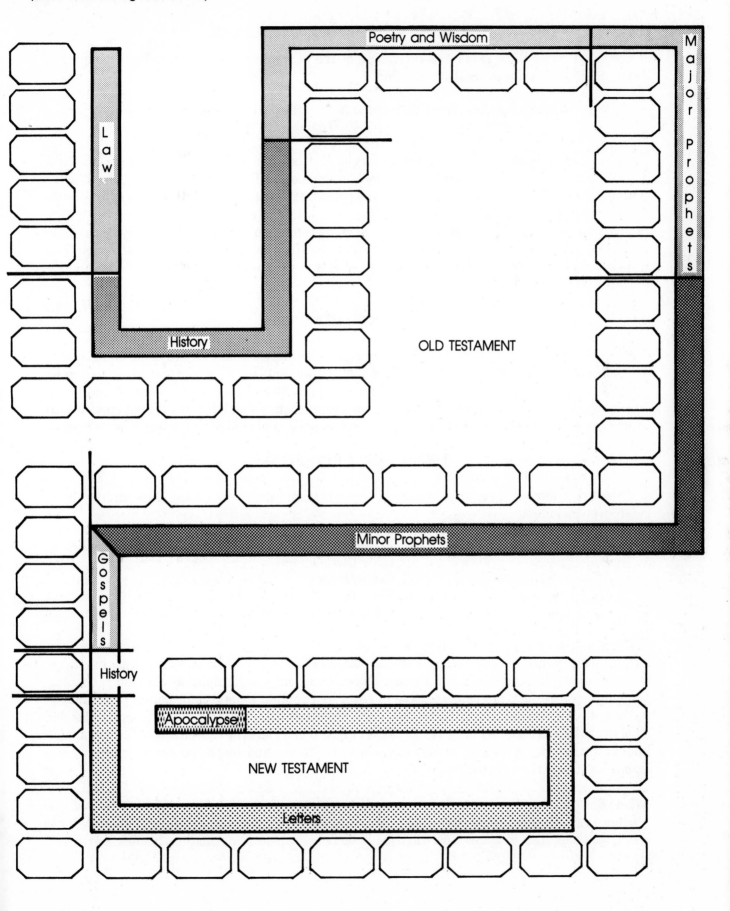

The Good News Bible lists cross-references at the beginning of a selection. For example, as cross-references to Luke 18:31-34, we find:

Jesus Speaks a Third Time about His Death......Heading of selection
(Matthew 20.17-19; Mark 10.32-34).......Cross-reference

We see here that we can find this same story in Matthew and in Mark. The wording is a little different, but the story is the same. If you look in some other Bibles, the New English Bible for example, you will find that you must look at the bottom of the page to find the cross-reference. To find the reference, you look at the bold print, 18:31-34. The cross-reference follows.

Younger students will find using the type of cross-reference that is illustrated by the sample from the *Good News Bible* easier to work with than the kind that is at the bottom of the page. The translation of the Bible that you are using may indicate to you the appropriate grade level at which to introduce this skill.

FOOTNOTES

Footnotes can provide interesting and important information when we are doing Bible study. To introduce this skill, we should first be sure that the students have learned how to use footnotes in school. They should know why footnotes are important and how to use them. Since many footnotes in the Bible refer to technical material, it is my feeling that it is probably not appropriate to introduce and to encourage the use of footnotes until senior high and adult class levels.

USING RESOURCE BOOKS

There are a number of resources that students will want to use when doing Bible study. These references include:

Atlases
Bible Dictionaries
Concordances
Word Books
Study Bibles

There are some very good children's editions of atlases, dictionaries, and concordances (see bibliography). Supplies of these books should be available in the classroom for students in grades five and above. Teachers will find these children's editions very helpful as they do their own planning because they are concise, easy to read, and contain helpful information. Introducing students to concordances, dictionaries, and maps after they have the skills to use them enables the students to be successful with the resources very quickly and lets the church school teacher spend time with the subject matter instead of taking time to try and teach the use of guide words, alphabetical order, or sequencing.

ATLASES

Bible atlases are different from many others because they contain a variety of other helpful resources in addition to maps. You will usually find geographical information, historical articles, chronology charts, time-lines, photographs, and illustrations that will provide information on a variety of subjects.

Using maps with students is a tricky business. Most students are introduced to the concept of maps in the first grade. However, it takes a long time for them to gain a global perspective—to be able to see a map and to translate what they see into actual space, location, and topography. Sometimes teachers do not realize that the students do not understand the maps on the same level as the teacher. Students may do well filling in an outline of a country or territory with the names of lakes, of cities, or of locations of important landmarks. When such an activity is done in the third and sometimes the fourth grades, the students are copying and understanding what is on the paper, but not necessarily translating what is on the paper into recognition of actual geographical location.

When introducing maps to the class, use simple ones. Take time to use a variety of resources to aid in the understanding of what you are trying to do—globes, atlases, world and regional maps, and pictures of the place(s) you are studying—so that the students can put the map you are using into context with the rest of the world and can begin to gain a sense of distance, of space, and of topography. Remember that many students as old as nine or ten years are still having trouble with north, south, east, and west directions.

Another confusing aspect of using biblical maps is that they are different from modern-day maps of the same territory. Boundaries have changed; names of places have changed. Being able to work with a map of the Holy Land as it appeared in the time of Moses, a map of the Holy Land as it appeared in the time of Jesus, and a map of the Holy Land as it appears today and to understand that all three maps are of the same physical area is a complicated task.

There are some activities we can do with maps at various grade levels. Here are a few. You will think of more as you look for creative and clear ways to work with maps with your students.

27. Students who need to touch and feel and manipulate in order to understand will enjoy making a relief map. Relief maps are fun to make. Their three-dimensional quality can give a very different perspective to the region you are studying from that of a flat map. Making hills and valleys, rivers and lakes, marking cities (even making walls to go around cities), painting deserts, and making trees and bushes to add in appropriate places can help students gain a much clearer idea of what the countryside is like. Have a variety of photographs of the area available so that students can see what the map should look like.

The most common way to make relief maps is to use papier-mâché and tempera paints. Most good craft books will have clear instructions for making and using papier-mâché. It is not a difficult craft, but it does take some planning and preparation. Making a relief map will take several weeks and some space. It is important for you to have a table or a place on the floor that will not be disturbed by other groups while your map is being created. When you finish the map you may want to share it with other classes or the entire congregation.

Relief maps can be made of a large region—like the Holy Land—or a small area—like the city of Jerusalem.

28. Besides using printed maps in books, students can gain a better sense of where things are if they are given papers with the outline of an area into which they can put the names of cities, rivers, lakes, and so on. You can use a spirit duplicator or copy machine to make copies of maps that show just the outline of the countries or territories you are working with. Or draw an outline on a transparency for the overhead projector and let students fill in the information. Or have teams of students work on creating a series of overlays with transparencies to show various important parts of a map study.

29. Make a puzzle out of a map. Mount a map on a light piece of cardboard or tag board. Protect the surface by covering with clear self-adhesive plastic. Use a sharp blade to cut the map into a variety of pieces. As students work to put the puzzle together, they will become familiar with the locations of cities, lakes, rivers, oceans, and other features of the territory shown on your map. The younger the student, the simpler the map should be and the fewer pieces in the puzzle.

30. Take a large piece of paper and draw the outline of the region that is the focus for your study. Use yarn, symbols that have been drawn on small pieces of paper, tissue paper, construction paper, and other objects to create your map. Yarn can be glued on the paper to show rivers, mountains, and boundaries. Tissue paper can be added for oceans, mountains or deserts. Symbols can indicate events. Pieces of paper with names of locations can be glued in the proper places. Use your imagination and the beautiful junk in your creative activities materials to create a map.

CONCORDANCES

A concordance is a listing in alphabetical order of key words used in the Bible. Concordances are used when you are trying to find a verse that you remember, but don't know where it is. If you can remember a key word from that verse, you can look in a concordance and find a listing of all the places where the word is used in the Bible. By scanning this list, you can find the verse you are looking for.

Students need to be able to identify key words in verses before they can successfully use a concordance. They also need to know how to scan a large body of text. Most students are comfortable with these two skills by the time they are in the fourth or fifth grades, but there are some who will not have much skill at either until sixth grade or later.

Let's look at a verse and see how we would find it in a concordance. Let's say that we remember these words:

Love God with all your heart, mind, and soul.

We identify *love* as a key word. When we look for the word *love* in the concordance, we find a long list of verses where *love* is used. As we scan, or skim through, this listing we come to:

"You shall love the Lord your God" Deut 6:5.

If we continue to skim until we come to the New Testament listings, we will come to:

"You shall love the Lord your God Mt 22:37
Mk 12:30
Lk 10:27

With this information, we can go to the Bible and find several places where this verse appears. The first thing we find is that we did not remember the words correctly and that the verse reads:

"Love the Lord your God with all your heart, with all your soul, and with all your mind."

There are two basic kinds of Bible concordance. Some concordances are very long and comprehensive. These contain all the listings of all the words in the Bible. They are helpful to those who are doing serious, heavy Bible study. There are also concise concordances which contain the most familiar, most important, and most representative passages related to key words from the Bible. This is the kind of concordance that is most helpful to students in church school.

As you look at various concordances, you will find that they use different styles for listing the references related to the key word. Some will spell out the key word; some will put the first letter of the word in italics and not spell out the word; some will use bold print for the key word. The above reference appeared in one concordance I looked in. Another concordance might list the reference like this:

"you shall *l*, the Lord your God Mt 22:37

If you use a concordance that uses this style, be sure to alert the students to the fact that the key word will not be spelled out in the listing of references.

31. One way to help students practice using the concordance is to make a list of several key verses that are included in your studies. Write out the verses in a column down one side of the paper and leave space next to each one for the student to write in the Biblical reference(s) for each verse. You could call this activity a "scavenger hunt." Include verses from previous lessons also.

The older the students, the more complicated and the longer you can make the scavenger hunt. You may want to include the above with directions for using other reference books in order to practice using a variety of resources. The scavenger hunt may include verses for which to find references, words for which to find definitions, and cities about which to find information. Having concordances, dictionaries, and atlases available, the student needs to decide which book to use in order to find the information needed to complete the scavenger hunt.

Scavenger Hunt
(Sample)

Where do the following verses appear in the Bible? Use a concordance to find biblical references for each of the verses. List the references you find next to the proper verse.

"Love the Lord your God with all your heart, with all your soul, and with all our mind." _____

_____

And the angel said, "Do not be afraid." _____

"Our Father who art in heaven, hallowed be thy name. . . ." _____

_____

"Some seeds fell in good soil and the plants sprouted, grew, and bore grain. Listen, then, if you have ears." _____

_____

BIBLE DICTIONARIES

Bible dictionaries include more than definitions of words. We will often find in Bible dictionaries brief articles giving background information about key words. Some Bible dictionaries are long and may be several volumes. Others are the size of a paperback book. Children will find the shorter, paperback dictionary helpful and non-threatening. But it would be a good idea to have a one-volume, larger dictionary available in the classroom to use when the smaller one does not give enough information. The teacher will need the larger dictionary to prepare for lessons.

32. A variety of activities can be created to practice using Bible dictionaries. One activity is to create a scavenger hunt (see previous activity) which would involve students in looking up key words from their lessons and in finding definitions or information about the words. Another choice would be to have students create a matching game where they would select a word, find the definition or information about the word, and put the word on one card and the information on another card. The cards could be collected and put near a bulletin board so that cards and information could be matched. Look through the activities we have already explored and adapt them to practicing the skill of using a Bible dictionary.

———

CONCLUSION

We have come to the end of this book. As you have read my ideas and seen suggestions for games, worksheets, and puzzles, you have been applying these to your church, your children, and your style of teaching. I hope I have caused you to think about your teaching and the use of Bibles in your church in a way different from before, and that you have been stimulated to create your own activities for teaching each of the skills.

As I sit at the computer typing these last few lines, I am thinking about you—the reader, the teacher, the director of Christian education, the pastor, the concerned friend of children—and praying that my book will be helpful to you as you open the Bible with your children. May God bless you in your ministry with the children of your church.

BIBLIOGRAPHY

Following is a listing of some of the books that may be helpful to you as you search for resources to aid in your teaching. In this list, you will find some children's Bible storybooks, Bibles that are appropriate for children, Bible dictionaries and atlases, and other resource books that have information about the Dead Sea Scrolls and the formation of the Bible. Some have excellent photographs that you will want to share with your students. Some of these books are no longer available in book stores, but they are the kinds of books you would find in your church, or public library. There are many, many other books available at your local religious book store. Use this list as a starting point when looking for helpful resources.

Allegro, John M. *The Dead Sea Scrolls*. Baltimore: Penguin Books, 1956.

——. *The People of the Dead Sea Scrolls: in Text and Pictures*. Toronto, Canada: Doubleday, 1958.

The Bible Companion. Nashville: Abingdon Press, 1985.

The Book of the Bible. Racine, Wis.: Western Publishing Co., 1973.

Cocagnac, A. M., and Rosemary Haughton. *Bible for Young Christians: The New Testament*. New York: Macmillan, 1967.

Doss, Helen. *Young Readers' Book of Bible Stories*. Nashville: Abingdon Press, 1971.

Drane, John. *Early Christians: Life in the First Years of the Church, an Illustrated Dictionary*. San Francisco: Harper & Row, 1982.

Everyday Life in Bible Times. Washington, D.C.: National Geographic Society, 1967.

Frank, Harry Thomas. *Discovering The Biblical World*. New York: Harper & Row, 1977.

Furnish, Dorothy J. *Exploring the Bible with Children*. Nashville: Abingdon, 1975.

——.*Living the Bible with Children*. Nashville: Abingdon, 1979.

Gardner, Joseph L., ed. *Atlas of the Bible: An Illustrated Guide to the Holy Land*. Reader's Digest Association, 1981.

Gehman, Henry Snyder, ed. *The New Westminster Dictionary of the Bible*. Philadelphia: Westminster Press, 1970.

Good News Bible, the Bible in Today's English Version. New York: American Bible Society, 1976.

Henderson, Robert and Ian Gould. *Life in Bible Times*. New York: Rand McNally, 1967.

Hughes, Gerald and Stephen Travis. *Harper's Introduction to the Bible*. San Francisco: Harper & Row, 1981.

International Children's Version: New Testament. Ft. Worth: Sweet Publishing Co., 1983.

Interpreter's Dictionary of the Bible, Five vols. Nashville: Abingdon Press, 1976.

Jones, Mary Alice. *Bible Stories: God at Work with Man*. Nashville: Abingdon Press, 1973.

——. *Know Your Bible*. New York: Rand McNally, 1965.

Maves, Paul and Mary. *Finding Your Way Through the Bible*. Nashville: Abingdon, 1971.

May, Herbert G. *Oxford Bible Atlas*. Oxford University Press, New York: 1984.

New Testament, Revised Standard Version. New York: American Bible Society, 1973.

Northcott, Cecil. *Bible Encyclopedia for Children*. Philadelphia: Westminster Press, 1964.

Photo-Guide to the New Testament. Hertfordshire, England: Lion Publishing Co., 1973.

Rappaport, Uriel. *The Story of the Dead Sea Scrolls*. New York: Harvey House, 1968.

RSV Handy Concordance. Grand Rapids: Zondervan Publishing House, 1972.

Smith, Barbara. *The Westminster Concise Bible Dictionary*. Philadelphia: Westminster Press, 1981.

Stoddard, Sandol. *The Doubleday Illustrated Children's Bible*. Garden City, N.J.: Doubleday, 1983.

Taize Picture Bible. Philadelphia: Fortress Press, 1969.

Terrien, Samuel. *The Golden Bible Atlas*. New York: Golden Books, 1957.

Trent, Robbie. *The Story of Your Very Own Bible*. Waco, Texas: Word Books, 1978.

Turner, Philip, ed. *Brian Wildsmith's Illustrated Bible Stories*. New York: Franklin Watts, 1969.

Young Readers Dictionary of the Bible. Nashville: Abingdon Press, 1969.

Wagerin, Walter, *My First Book About Jesus*. San Francisco: Rand McNally, 1984.

Filmstrips

How We Got the Bible, a series of four filmstrips.

The Translations of the Bible
The Bible Comes into Being
The Manuscripts of the Bible
The Bible and Recent Discoveries

Produced by Broadman Films, Nashville, 1972.